COLLATERAL DAMAGE

COLLATERAL DAMAGE

✦

The John List Story

John List
With Austin Goodrich

iUniverse, Inc.
New York Lincoln Shanghai

COLLATERAL DAMAGE
The John List Story

iUniverse books may be ordered through booksellers or by contacting:

iUniverse
2021 Pine Lake Road, Suite 100
Lincoln, NE 68512
www.iuniverse.com
1-800-Authors (1-800-288-4677)

ISBN-13: 978-0-595-39536-1 (pbk)
ISBN-13: 978-0-595-67724-5 (cloth)
ISBN-13: 978-0-595-83935-3 (ebk)
ISBN-10: 0-595-39536-8 (pbk)
ISBN-10: 0-595-67724-X (cloth)
ISBN-10: 0-595-83935-5 (ebk)

Printed in the United States of America

Dedicated to my father and mother who raised me in a loving Christian home, and to all family members made victims by my sinful actions.

—John E. List

Contents

Introduction

It is apparent to me that after waiting this long to write about the tragedy that fell on my family because of my actions, it is appropriate to explain why this book should be written. It may be helpful to psychiatrists and moralists (Christians and others) and I hope will ease the pain caused by my actions to the friends and relatives of my victims.

I grew up in a friendly, industrious and mutually supportive community of first and second generation German-Americans in Bay City, Michigan. From the very beginning, I was immersed in the conservative religious culture of the Lutheran Church (Missouri Synod). In grade school I was a B average pupil and as her only child the focus of my mother's love and attention. As a registered nurse sensitive to the real threat of polio in those days, she was undoubtedly overprotective in raising me.

Faced by the intellectual challenge posed by Latin, history and math I excelled in High School and gained recognition as a member of the National Honor Society.

I survived my military experience, including 41 days of combat and two days as a prisoner of war in Germany, without any known disability. Only much later did I learn that I had incurred post traumatic stress disorder caused by combat in World War II.

My university education, return to the Army (this time as an officer), marriage and employment experience further shaped my personality for good and ill in a way that led to disaster. After a succession of professional and marital setbacks I finally reached the point of no return, when I despaired of ever being able to provide for my family. It was then that I realized I had to act to avoid the loss of our home, all of our earthly possessions and our established social position. Once the action die was cast and set in motion by irreversible resolve, the murder of my family and my flight played out in a series of ad hoc decisions. There was no need for any detailed planning of the scenario, because I was convinced that I would quickly be captured and executed.

Although I had chosen Denver as my destination, the route to be followed was dictated by the situation as the day ran its course. The generation of a new name, social security card, driver's license, occupation and social life developed as circumstances dictated. Thus, there was no rationally predictable course for the law enforcement people to follow, and the hit and miss nature of my second life kept it going.

My arrest by the FBI, incarceration, trial and transfer to a maximum security prison required additional adjustments, which are covered in my book.

Preface

John List and Austin Goodrich, who collaborated in the writing of this biography, were cast in similar molds. Both were born in the late summer of 1925 into solid middle class, church-going families in mid-size Michigan cities located about 100 miles apart. They both enlisted in the Army in late 1943 and were assigned to the 86th Blackhawk Division where they served as gravel-clutchers (infantrymen) in the same platoon for the next 26 months before returning to civilian life via Camp McCoy, Wisconsin in the spring of 1946. Both survived 42 days of combat in Germany, were awarded Combat Infantry Badges, and later Bronze Star medals before being shipped to the Philippines as WWII came to an end. The platoon mates returned to civilian life and with G.I. Bill assistance earned their bachelor degrees at the University of Michigan in 1949. At that point the lives of these two members of what TV journalist Tom Brokaw dubbed in his book *The Greatest Generation* moved in different directions.

Goodrich became a radio reporter and free lance journalist before embarking on a career as a case officer in the Central Intelligence Agency. John List took a masters degree in business administration and after serving as a commissioned finance officer in the Army during the Korean War began crunching numbers as a Certified Public Accountant. Both men were married twice and sired a total of eight children while moving to a dozen different locations. Both men used aliases: Goodrich to conceal his true identity from various foreign security services and his communist recruitment targets; List to disassociate himself from the person whose picture appeared on post office walls across the country, wanted for the murder of his mother, wife and three children in 1971.

Apart from casual meetings when their paths crossed in Ann Arbor, List and Goodrich met for the first time since the war in the visitation area at New Jersey State Prison in Trenton in 1990. List had only just begun to serve a prison sentence of five consecutive life terms for the murder of his family. In place of a handshake and spoken greetings, the convict and his visitor could only press their hands together on either side of a cold glass partition that separated their worlds. A broad smile shattered the once gentle, now hardening face of John List. He picked up the phone receiver, which promptly slipped out of his grasp and fell noisily to the counter. Although the sound failed to carry through the window, it drew the attention of the guard, who came to see what had happened. The accident also served as fresh evidence of List's continued difficulty in physical coordination, which helped to bridge the forty-five-year interval between meetings of these former comrades in arms. Still the meeting was strained as neither man knew what to talk about. So they retreated into the world of shared trivia: how right tackle Goodrich had felt when his high school football team suffered its only defeat of the season at the hands of List's Bay City eleven; and how List felt when his Wehrmacht captors had discussed whether to shoot him and his ten captured comrades on a Ruhr hillside. Moving uneasily from the past to the uneasy present the convict and his visitor discussed how it might be possible for them to work together to correct the egregious errors appearing in books about List's life that had sprung up like mushrooms after the rain since his trial. List hoped that this could be done in a way that would financially benefit his wife, Delores Miller Clark. As the innocent wife of a man known to her as Bob Clark, Delores became the victim of media rape after his arrest and went into seclusion. She later declined any financial help and quietly got a divorce.

Thirty minutes after their conversation started, just as it had reached a comfort zone, it was abruptly ended by the sound of an alarm. The telephone went dead. When the guard moved towards him, a haunted expression clouded List's face and he nervously snapped to attention, awaiting orders. Goodrich waved a limp salute, List nodded. In the reception hall where he went to collect the belongings that he had deposited there (including a ballpoint pen and writing tablet), the sergeant in charge said there had been a mistake and that Goodrich could return to have additional time for his visit. But it was too late. The fragile strands of rapport that had been braided in the shared stress and horror of war had been torn asunder. "Red" Goodrich walked out into the rain-drenched parking lot, looked back at the tall brick walls, and cried.

Before leaving the prison in a taxi, Goodrich glanced through an official pamphlet, which proclaims that "the new design is an example of a fine balance which has been struck between security and the overall community environment." In actual fact, the dark red brick façade of the three-story new section sdtruck the visitor as downright pleasing to the eye in contrast with the surrounding neighborhood, a depressing mosaic of inner city blight, the ugly residue of America's shiny new Information Age. Abandoned smoke-grayed buildings that not so long ago housed muscular factories silently mock the message of a nearby billboard: "Trenton Makes—The World Takes." Their faces pockmarked with broken windows, these Rust Belt custodians stand guard over the neighborhoods they once nourished. It's a silent place. Wood framed row houses stand on both sides of dirty streets lined with crumbled curbs. Their faded yellow paint is peeling, the white window trim is gone. Some second story windows are without glass, others are boarded over. Hardy gray-green weeds struggle to sprout through the surface of hardpan front lawns, and there are no children to be seen. Here and there young men with half-naked black bodies are perched gracefully on porch rails staring with empty eyes into the street waiting for who knows what or whom. Maybe they feel envy for the secure life of their incarcerated brothers and sisters down the block. Maybe John List is well off right where he is. But just then there comes into view through the taxi window a blue and white sign at the corner of Greenwood and Hamilton. Its hand-painted message reads "Welcome to Our Neighborhood." Sad. But somehow hopeful.

In addition to the talks the writer and convict had in prison, the information contained in this biography has drawn on a dozen years of correspondence, trial transcripts and the oral and written history supplied by family and friends of John List. Questions that may emerge regarding the fairness of his trial and sentencing, and the quality of his defense counsel will be left to the informed judgment of the reader.

Having refused to participate in most print and TV exploitation of his murders, List hopes that an objective depiction of the circumstances of his life may produce a better understanding of this American tragedy, why it happened, how the conditions that produced it could have been altered to reach a happier ending. By extension, he hopes that his story may be helpful in suggesting ways to overcome the demons of violence besetting our society, including the early diagnosis and treatment of post traumatic stress disorder.

List will receive no financial benefit from this work, which is the copyrighted property of his comrade in arms and friend, Austin "Red" Goodrich.

1

The Early Years

I, John Emil List, was born on September 17, 1925, in Bay City, Michigan. I was baptized in a German language service of the Mr. Zion Lutheran Church (Missouri Synod) in the name of Johann Emil List.

My father, John Frederich List, was born in 1864, one of eleven children of whom seven survived infancy. The high rate of infant mortality was common in those days. So also were marriages among family members. My mother, Alma Maria Barbara List, who married John Frederich a year after the death of his first wife, was the grand daughter of her husband's father, which made them second cousins.

The List family has been traced back to 1690 in the town of Rosstal in the Franconian district of Bavaria in southern Germany. It is quite possible that they were refugees who fled to Bavaria from Hungary during the religious wars of the 17th Century, in which case, I might be a distant relative of the famed composer, Franz Liszt. This might explain my lifelong love of classical music and my talent for playing the violin in several different orchestras all the way through high school.

It is also possible though equally unlikely that I could be a distant relation of the noted German army general Wilhelm List, who had a Bavarian regiment named after him in which Corporal Adolph Hitler had served in WW I, and who rose to the rank of Field Marshall in Hitler's Wehrmacht during World War II. My 86th Blackhawk Division squad leader in that war, Joe Heitman, posited that my high-ranking military genes may have fuelled my ambition to rise above my private first class rank and motivated me to re-enlist in the Army during the Korean War. In a letter to "Red" Goodrich, who was a light machine gun squad leader in the same platoon, Heitman wrote of me: [In WW II], "*John was in the ASTP Program aiming at training to be an engineering officer. Instead, he spent the war as an enlisted man in the infantry. When the Korean War came along, John enlisted as a Lieutenant in the Finance Department, because he felt compelled to get a*

commission and be a leader. In his own mind John expected to be a leader or man-
ager, for which he was not fitted."

I have to point out that in the German language, "list" means cunning or shrewdness. Was it a disingenuous personality trait derived from my family name that enabled me to elude capture for nearly eighteen years after the murder of my mother, wife and three young children in Westfield, New Jersey, in1971? Or was it, to the contrary, the absence of an elaborate scheme that enabled me to evade the law and calmly go about forging a second life while my pursuers got stuck in a tangled web of rational forensic probabilities?

From the ethereal clouds of speculation, let's return to the turnip and parsnip roots of the List family on Planet Earth. By 1845, the Lutherans in the farming village of Rosstal in mainly Roman Catholic Bavaria, were encouraged by their church to emigrate to America where they would establish communities in the wilderness to serve as bases for missionary work among the Indians. Another good reason to move was undoubtedly supplied by a desire by many Rosstalers, to avoid compulsory military service in the Bavarian armed forces. The first set-tlement took root in Frankenmuth, Michigan, at the base of the thumb and index finger in the mitten-shaped state. The name was German for "Courage of the Franconians." Other Michigan communities established by the immigrants from Rosstal were Frankenhilf (Help of the Franconians), Frankentrost (Conso-lation of the Franconians) and Frankenlust (Delight of the Franconians).

In these ethnic enclaves, all of the immigrants spoke German (it was said that the dogs even barked in German) and most attended Lutheran churches where services were conducted in the German language until the late 19930's.

My paternal grandfather, Johann List (1816-1882) married Marie Barbara Lotter in 1845 on the North Sea shortly after embarking from the northern Ger-man port of Bremen aboard the ship *Caroline.* They were joined by several other unwed couples who had postponed their nuptials to avoid the expense of wed-ding ceremonies, which typically lasted several days in Rosstal. That way, the emigrants cold use the money saved to pay for their passage and have funds left over to buy some fertile farmland at nominal homestead prices from the govern-ment and set up housekeeping in the New World.

The List party, which included a Lutheran pastor, several married couples and a bachelor, landed in New York, where they were processed through Ellis Island. They then took a boat up the Hudson and a barge on the Erie Canal to another boat, which transported them to the port of Detroit. After a few days of needed rest in Detroit, the group traveled by train to Saginaw and finally trekked through the woods some 15 mils to the settlement of Frankenmuth. Following a time-honored practice of the early pioneers, the Rostall settlers first built a log church and only later built their homes and a school. There came to be so many List families in the farming community that it was necessary to distinguish them by their locations or occupations; thus, my ancestors, who built their house across from the church, became known as the Kirchen Lists (Church Lists). The settlers did some missionary work among the Ojibwa Indians, but this activity declined after the government moved these tribes on to a reservation near Owosso, some 50 miles away. The missionary work ws not totally abandoned, however, and I recall havingf visited the reservation several times for church services there when I was about five years old.

When John Frederick List was about 18 years old, he moved to Bay City to work for his brother who owned a grocery store there. My father bought the store when his brother moved out west, where both weather and living conditions were somewhat easier than on the west bank of the west branch of the Saginaw River, where even a store owner had to work long and hard to remain financially solvent. I recall how my father told of having to walk to classes in a business school five miles away from his home to learn how to operate his business more efficiently. Thanks more to hard work than formal education, John Frederick List eventually built a home just a block from his original location, that encompassed three building lots on Saltzburg Ave. Founded by immigrants from Salatzburg, Austria, this area in the early 1900's became a part of Bay City to which it was linked by a bridge between Salzburg Ave. and Pulaski Ave. over the Saginaw River. To the north of Salzburg, which retained its ethnic identity long after its incorporation into Bay City, was an area known as Frenchtown, with quite different ethnic roots located on Saginaw Bay. During the 1930's I remember how my father and I used to go to the docks there to buy fresh fish for dinner. This happy memory was only one of many I shared with my Dad, who was sixty years old when I was born.

The best of times with Dad were when we were doing things together. The first time I remember is when he had set up the small store selling candy, tobacco products, magazines, etc. These were times when I was at the store with him. We weren't ever very busy, so we had time to talk. It must have been "small talk," as I don't remember anything special. In the summertime, I would join Dad on the porch. I would often have him tell me about his earlier life. During these times he told me about why his parents came to America, and about the Indians that lived across the river. Also, how he hauled water on a horse-drawn wagon for the cement used to construct the St. Lawrence Church, and how he used to walk to school (a mile and a half each way) with the Pastor's son. He told me about how he came to Bay City, worked for his brother and later got his own store, and how he used to go to the farmers' market early in the morning to buy produce for the store.

Then later, when he had the broker route, I was happy when I could help him in various ways. This included going to Saginaw to buy noodles. In Bay City, we went to the Golden Pickle factory to buy pickles and relish products. At different locations, we also bought freshly-ground horseradish, which brought tears to my eyes, and peanuts, which we re-packaged for sale from 30 lb. cartons into 10 and 20 pound bags.

During vacations from school, I also went with Dad on the route. I was then able to go to the car and bring in the order for each store. I especially liked our trips to Midland, Michigan. This happened about every other week. Normally, Midland was a pleasant town. However, when the humidity was high, the smell emanating from the Dow Chemical plant was awful.

Our special treat was to buy two Hostess five-cent "Twinkies" and later 10-cent pies. We would stop at the side of the road and eat them and talk about the day's business.

Once I was upset by an experience with my Dad that involved killing. It happened when I was about five years old in a building behind our house that had once been used as a barn before being converted into a garage for a car. On the south side of this garage there stood a smaller structure used as a chicken coop. One day my Dad took me out there to watch him chop the head off a chicken. When the beheaded fowl flapped its wings and ran around, I was scared to death, until Dad assured me there was nothing to be afraid of.

As far as I can remember, most of the time I spent with Dad was quality time. He only had to spank me once, when I earned it by being unruly in church.

The only other time I can remember being unhappy with my father was when he refused to let me use the car to have a date with Serene Morris. I finally got to use the car, and I don't know what had happened to change Dad's mind, but it left me with a kindly feeling towards him. My Dad had Jewish friends and knew that Serene's father was Jewish and that he ran a grocery store across the river. I don't know if he had some reason to dislike Mr. Morris or if he simply didn't want me to get involved with a non-Lutheran. Our date was certainly very tame. In fact, I later wondered if Serene probably wasn't bored by it. She was pleasant the entire time. She went to college in Ohio and promised to write to me. While I was at the University of Wisconsin (late 1943) I wrote to her home several times, but I never received a reply. That's how my romance with Serene ended. I never went to a class reunion, so I never again saw her.

All in all, m Dad wa a kindly man, the same as the rest of my relatives on both sides. They must have retained some of the Bavarian *gemuetlichkeit*.

After ten years in the New Jersey State Prison, I can still recall quite clearly what it was like to grow up as the only child in a loving family in Bay City, Michigan. My parents often showed that they loved each other. They would do this by hugging and kissing at various times. Often they pulled me close to them so that I was a part of the hugging.

While Dad had the dry goods store, Mother often worked there. During the hard times of the Great Depression, I didn't ever hear them having any arguments about our financial situation. As I grew older I realized that at times we had been in very tight financial straits, but these bad times were never discussed, never gave rise to arguments or complaints. My parent at one point remodeled out house to create an apartment on the second floor to get rental income, and I was moved into a room on the ground floor that had earlier served as a parlor.

I remember how ice used to be delivered to the house and we used an icebox late into the 30's because my folks couldn't afford a refrigerator. We couldn't even afford a telephone. To reach us, the caller the caller had to call the Loessel family across the street and these good folks had to come over to get us. When Mother had to make a call, she had to go over to these neighbors for that purpose. Even considering what we had to do without, I came to realize that we were better off than some people in the depression years that preceded World War II.

Fortunately, my parents had simple tastes, which enabled us to live without several things that other had to spend money on. For example, we didn't attend any movies, which were frowned on by the church. But we did have a Victrola that we used to play thick records. All that I can remember of the music was Harry Lauder, an Irish tenor, some Susa marches and some songs with Spanish themes such as La Paloma. (At my Aunt Gustie's, I enjoyed listening to Strauss waltzes, especially "The Blue Danube," and religious hymns, my favorite of which was "Beautiful Savior.") We also listened to some radio programs, including The Lone Ranger, a favorite of mine. On Sunday evenings we listened to the Detroit Symphony Orchestra, sponsored by the Ford Motor Co..

In truth, my social life all the way through high school was pretty much limited to a tightly drawn circle of close relatives and church members. I never went to school dances, but I do remember dancing—probably more like skipping—around the May pole at Riegel School Kindergarten. This was a memorable experience, because I had very little chance to play with other kids. No doubt one reason for this was my mother's being more protective than other mothers in the area.

The first instance of this I remember occurred at an extended family picnic easrt of Frankenmuth on the Tibiawasi River when I was about three years old. My older cousins were playing baseball and I was having a great time running around with my young cousins and *their* friends. I wasn't used to playing with so many kids my age. It was a warm day, and Mother stopped my playing because as a nurse she saw of signs of my getting overheated. As a kid I always got red as a beet and sweat a lot. Mother was also probably concerned with the danger of polio meningistis, which was widely associated with the dog days of summer. The dread disease of polio got widespread public attention, not least because of publicity surrounding it most prominent victim, President Franklin D. Roosevelt.

Throughout my life, even when I was in my forties and we were living in Westfield, Mother reminded me to bundle up against winter cold, be sure to wear rubbers when it rained and goulashes when it snowed. (I did not, as some writers have claimed, mow the lawn wearing a three-piece suit. I never owned a vest.)

As a matter of fact, I had no regular playmates in my neighborhood and rarely stayed after school to play sports on the playground with kids of my age. Apart from travel with my father, including a drive to Toledo to buy coffee for his store, and a bus trip to Chicago with my mother, the outer limits of my childhood world never extended beyond the city limits of Bay City. My social life into my late teens, like many of my relatives, peaked at church festivals in Frankenmuth, a town 25 miles from Bay City, where the List family had originally settled and many continued to reside. It was there that the Fourth of July was celebrated with a children's festival known as Kinderfest, which featured a parade through the town followed by a religious service, children's games and a sit-down luncheon catered by the Ladies Aid Group, which was mainly for adults. In August there was Missions Festival with Church services, and collections that were designated for Lutheran missionary work. Both of these festivals featured an abundance of German cuisine and the sale of beer supplied bfy the local Frankenmuth and Geyer's breweries. During children's games I remember how I'drun around with my cousins and their friends. I always got red as a beet and sweat a lot.

The festivals always ran well into the night. On one occasion when I was abfout ten years old, I was accidentally abandoned when all of the departing revelers assumed that I had been driven back to my aunt's house in someone else's car. When all of the cars had left, there was nothing left to do but to talk to the sheriff. Everyone know Aunt Gustie, (Alma List's sister, Augusta) so there was no problem in being delivered to the right home.

This was not to be the last time that John List would quietly disappear without leaving a trace of his presence.

In my early youth, I was generally absent from the vacant lots that served as playing fields where my boy cousins and others of my age spent most of their free time emulating their Michigan sports heroes, notably slugger Hank Greenberg and Second Baseman Charlie Gehringer of the American League champion Detroit Tigers, and the Michigan Wolverines Tom Harmon and Forest Evashevski. I was quite obviously ill-equipped for active participation in the world of sports. I was tall for my age, reaching six feet in high school, and gangly. Moreover, there always seemed to be a problem in communication between my active brain and my un-coordinated extremities. I never stumbled over my own feet, but I often felt that I might easily do so if I wasn't careful. Thus, in choose-up-sides games, I was always the last kid to be picked, and often I wasn't chosen by either team captain, so I joined the last team to choose by default. I disliked gym classes and skipped them whenever I could think up an excuse to do so.

It's supposed to be easy, but I even had trouble learning to ride a bike. Sometime between the ages of 10 and 12, Herbert Bach, the son of a schoolteacher, dropped by the house, perhaps at Dad's behest, to instruct me. The lesson went poorly, and my teacher gave up my education as a lost cause. Shortly thereafter I displayed greater aptitude in learning how to drive a car. Dad gave me lessons in our 1925 Chevy at the Fairgrounds, where I could practice with little chance of encountering another car in preparation for getting a driver's license art the then legal age of fourteen. After my first lesson, I proudly announced to mother: "Now I am a man!" Only much later did I learn that there is more to being a man than driving a car.

My physical limitations did not prevent me from working as a caddy at the Country Club one summer. I had learned this ancient skill during some happy times spent with some aunts, uncles and cousins at beautiful Houghton Lake in central Michigan, where the weather always seems cooler and less humid than in Bay City. After fishing in the early morning hours, my older cousins, Ralph and Harold List, would invite me to join them for a found of golf—as a caddy. I enjoyed this.

The closest I came to participation in a team sport was when I accepted an invitation to try out for the junior high school football team. This opportunity fizzled, however, when my parents refused to give their consent. In a way this was fortunate as a face-saving out, for I seriously doubt that I could have made the team. In any case, my father, who spent his life working to support his families, had never had time to get involved in sports, even as a spectator. Perhaps mindful of my physical limitations, Fred had discouraged me from participating in football by recounting the story of a son of a friend of his who had been left to walk with a permanent limp because of a football injury. Mother's experience as a registered nurse, including a stint at the VA Hospital in Battle Creek, MI, where amputees were treated during World War II, had sensitized her to the long-term problems associated with physical injuries. Hence, her insistence that her son should take care to avoid injury. "Be careful" was her watchword.

If a cautious upbringing contributed to my sitting out most sport activities, it failed to prevent a few health problems. In the fall of 1943 I scraped my face and arms rather badly when my scooter spun out of control and I was thrown to the sidewalk. Shortly thereafter I came down with a mastoid infection, which my mother, contrary to the doctor's judgment, attributed to my accident. As always happened when I was ill, I was moved from my upstairs bed room to my parent's bed on the ground floor. I was joined there by my mother while father moved to an upstairs bedroom to sleep. Since this was before the sulfa and antibiotic "miracle drugs," it was necessary to perform surgery or let the disease run its course, which entailed the risk of permanent brain damage or death.

While I was at home prior to the operation, I thought that I saw the Devil and his horde emerge from the pendulum clock that hung in my folk's bedroom.

The operation involved chiseling out some bone behind my right ear, which left a scar that was cited as an identifying mark on FBI public enemy poster that appeared on post office walls across the country.

Surgical procedures sometimes became uncomfortable topics for dinner table conversation usually centered on mother's experience in the operating room. At times, my sympathy for the patients brought me to the brink of passing out. Once I had to leave the table and lie down to regain my composure. Years later I had a similar reaction in a dentist's office when my wife, Helen, had some teeth extracted.

In Bay City Central High School, I followed a college prep program, concentrating on courses in Latin, math, chemistry and physics. At a relatively young age I had decided to pursue a career as a research chemist instead of studying for the ministry as had been suggested to me shortly after my Confirmation by Pastor Mayer. If the first seventeen years of a person's life can be summed up in a few words, I guess I had it right when I wrote t my Army platoon mate: *I'm sorry there isn't more to tell, Red, but I guess my life just wasn't very exciting.*

2

World War II

On Sunday, December 7, 1941, I was listening to a N.Y. Philharmonic concert when the broadcast was suddenly interrupted with the announcement of the Japanese attack on Pearl Harbor. It had been a quiet afternoon. Mrs. Born sat with mother in the living room and Dad was at church attending a congregation voters' meeting. It was a sunny day, warm for that time of year, but an ominous chill ran through me.

It wasn't long before the shock of the event gave way to excitement and a sense of national purpose, patriotism. In practically no time, it seemed that all Americans came together in a determination to pay back the Japs for their sneak attack. Secretary of State Cordell Hull's remark to the Japanese so-called "peace ambassadors" that this was a most detestable way for their government to act understated the feelings of the American public.

In Battle Creek, a hundred miles or so to the southwest, a 17-year-old boy who was soon to become an Army buddy of mine, also recalled Pearl Harbor Day with excitement. He wrote in his memoirs: "Never was there a more carefree teenager than the kid with a hard-on under his Macintkosh perusing nude photos in a pocket-size magazine kept for special clients at the newsstand where I worked weekends in an open arcade. It was December 7, 1941, and the little radio behind the counter announced the bombing of Pearl Harbor. A surge of excitement announced my coming involvemenet.

"At the time, we kids thought that war was heroic, romantic, sorta sexy. Okay, so the Germans in *All Quiet on the Western Front* weren't exactly reveling in those muddy trenches. But then, they were only Krauts with pointy helmets, and Krauts aren't supposed to have any fun anyway. The real heroes of war were like Errol Flynn in *Dawn Patrol*. What a man! As oil spattered his windshield but never soiled the white satin scarf that fly out behind him, Errol smiled. The air-cooled machine guns kept spitting their lethal bullets through the prop of his Spad fighter plane. Flynn's smile broadened as the Fokker with Maltese crosses on its tail and wings began to leave trail of smoke before spinning to the ground. And Flynn gallantly saluted his fallen foe. Ah, yes, that the way wars are fought! Or so we thought. Boy, were we wrong!"

I thought like Red, and I couldn't wait to enlist ("for the duration plus six months") in the Army Student Training Program (ASTP). I was still 17 years old, freshly graduated from high school. I continued to stock shelves and bag groceries at Krogers through the summer while attending Bay City Junior College to give my college education a jump start. On the day after Labor Day, I left Bay City for what turned out to be the duration of my life. On my way to the University of Wisconsin to begin my brief service as a soldier-student in the US Army, I stopped for a family-warm overnight visit at the home of Uncle Frank and Aunt Ida in Chicago.

The trip to Madison (Wisconsin) was uneventful. I joined another ASTP reservist for lunch, using Army meal vouchers. In Madison ("Mad City" as it's known by students there) we studied engineering courses for a semester before being transferred to active duty status. After a 10-day furlough, I reported to Ft. Sheridan, Illinois, to be inducted into the real Army six months to the day after I'd enlisted in the ASTP student-soldier program. After a three-day pass, when I surprised my parents by showing up on their doorstep after they had gone to bed, I was shipped out to Fort Benning for basic training.

Among my memories from this training was a particular platoon sergeant who had to hold the Guiness World Record for the use of foul language. This tall, red-faced hillbilly cold never complete a sentence without including at least one cuss word. He sometimes found it necessary to squeeze a profanity inside one of his rarely used polysyllables. Thus, to underscore an assurance of heavy punishment for those who might disobey an order, he would shout: "If you don't pass this inspection, I'll guaran-goddamned tee ya…." We college boys learned early on that rank had its privilege, and that higher rank did not necessarily correlate with either higher formal education or even proper upbringing.

I remember the first pass that we received. We had been in basic training for about six weeks before several of us took the bus into Columbus, Georgia. We were prohibited from going across the river to Phoenix City, Alabama, a place known as Sin City for good reason. After a pleasant walk around town we found a good restaurant and enjoyed a delicious steak dinner. There wasn't beer to be had, but we drank plenty of milk. When I told Red about this, he said he wished he had drunk "cow juice" in Columbus. He had gone into town with a buddy with the idea of downing a couple of mixed drinks, but this was impossible, because state liquor laws forbade the sale of mixed drinks in restaurants. It was okay, however, to buy a fith at a state liquor store and take your brown-bagged potable into a restaurant where they would serve set-ups and you mixed your own drinks right there at your table. Thanks to this counter-productive law, Red and his companion had—naturally—downed an entire fifth before staggering back to camp. Red showed up late for reveille and his pal was found worshipping at the enamel Buddha (as toilet bowls were called) in the latrine.

In early March, after a day on the firing range, we were advised that the ASTP program was no longer in the business of sending young men back to college. Instead, we were to become real soldiers in an infantry division, the recently activated 86th Blackhawk Division in Camp Livingston, Louisiana. Real tears were shed in the barracks that night, but most of us were happy to be assigned to a line outfit. Now at last we would get Infantry blue piping on our caps, and red-and-black shoulder patches on our Class A uniforms to show our pride in belonging to a real, honest-to-goodness regular Army division.

Just a month after our arrival at Camp Livingston, we were given furloughs. From camp we were bused into nearby Alexandria, a city whose 50,000 civilians were outnumbered by Army and Air Force personnel stationed in the surrounding area. (Small wonder that girls were kept behind double-locked doors beyond the reach of soldiers that inundated the streets of this fine Old South city on weekends.)

At home I found that Dad no longer had his broker business, and he didn't feel very well. This may have been partly due to his worrying about me and other relatives who were off serving in the armed forced.

Dad was quite concerned about the name of our division, "Blackhawk," which he thought must be some sort of special forces unit more exposed to danger than regular infantry. At one point, Dad asked his son Will if there wasn't a way to be exempted from military service. He thought that the Lutheran Church could get its members exempted as conscientious objectors. This rather surprised me as Dad had told me that at the time of the Spanish-American war, when he was 34, he considered enlisting in the army, but they weren't taking married men. Anyway, my half-brother assured Dad that the Church would not issue such a statement to help its members sidestep our duty.

Blackhawk Recollections

From the very beginning, the 86th Division was an anomaly. Originally established as a reserve division in World War I, it was comprised mainly of conscripts from Illinois, Wisconsin and Minnesota. The outfit was named after a famous military leader of the Sauk Indians, but its emblem—a black hawk on a red shied—resembled the Prussian eagle that adorned the helmets of German troops. Lest our bird be confused with theirs, the letters B and H appeared on a red shield in the center of our division emblem. Although the division got to France, it never fought as a unit, because its personnel were assigned as replacements for line units. Thus, the 86th never quite gained an identity of its own.

A war later, after the division moved from Camp Howze in Texas to Camp Livingston, an identity crisis of another kind arose. Apart from a handful of Regular Army stalwarts, the cadre of non-commissioned officers from Howze consisted of draftees with only a year or so of Army service. Graduates of the school of hard knocks, few of these corporals and sergeants had ever received a high school diploma; many had their formal education terminated in the sixth grade or earlier.

At the bottom of the ladder were the privates and privates first class, most of whom were either college boys or high school graduates headed for college in the ASTP program. Their lowly ranks were augmented by thousands of Air Force cadets, who saw their Dawn Patrol dreams go down in flames in the swamps of Louisiana. Our country needed more foot soldiers than it needed scholars and aviators. Thus, the stage was set for turning Plato's prescription for an ideal society, Utopia, upside down. The more intelligent, better educated members stood at the bottom of the social mix while the less educated, libido-driven members of the division were put in positions of command.

A recipe for disaster? Not at all. By virtue of some weird social alchemy, the Blackhawk composition worked. Mutual distrust was somehow transmuted into a pervasive climate of mutual trust and, yes, even admiration that bonded the most disparate of cultural backgrounds into a unified and smoothly functioning whole.

I suppose because of my stiff and structured upbringing I adapted rather easily to the requirements of army life. By and large I accepted discipline as a necessary for an effective fighting force. Not all of my comrades shared this view. In fact, some of my fellow privates asserted their human worth by demonstrating a high degree of independence. On one hot, humid day Pfc Lothrop "Bud" Mittenthal got into a confrontation with Sgt. Victor Renda, an Italo-American from Des Moines. Although, as a civilian, would have had nothing but contempt for any man who helped a wife with housework, he had become a neat-freak in the Army. Every morning he wakened his charges in the eight-man wood and tarpaper hut with the exhortation: "all right, snap shit, let's get going and clean this place up." One morning the snap shit command caused Mittenthal to fix his superior with his beady, baleful eyes and observe quite calmly: "Sergeant Renda, you are a red-assed baboon." Renda jumped back jumped back, eyes wide open, but said nothing. Later in the day, he asked Red Goodrich in private, "What is wrong with that guy? Is he crazy or something?" Pfc Goodrich replied, "Yeah, you gotta watch him. He's a math major at Cal Tech." Sgt. Renda who had quit school at a tender age to work as a croupier in a Des Moines gambling establishment silently turned away with his dark brow still deeply furled.

I have to characterize my military training performance as diligent but unlucky. Sort of like the rest of my life. For example:

The weapons platoon, including the 60 mm mortar squad in which I served as assistant gunner, had somehow goofed up on an earlier field exercise and we had to repeat the drill on Saturday morning. We were ordered to set up the mortar in what turned out to be an undesirable location. The base plate was put down on a patch of wet ground with a tree branch directly overhead. We soon found out why it was unwise to put the base plate on soft ground, where it could change direction after the first round was fired, and under a tree branch which the shell could strike and explode. And so it happened. After the first round was fired, the base plate shifted and the second round hit a tree branch and exploded directly over head. The tree burst could have killed all of us, but fortunately the only near-victim was Steve Jarvis, an assistant light machine gunner whose back pack was penetrated by a piece of shrapnel that luckily came to rest on a metal rivet on the raincoat packed inside it.

During another training exercise I was assigned the unenviable task of firing a flame-thrower against an "enemy" pill box in the hills of Camp St. Louis Obispo, CA.. A squad mate, "Rusty" Hayes ran up to the target to toss a satchel charge into its opening when I prematurely let off a mighty blast of flaming liquid gas that very nearly seared off his canvas leggings. Soon thereafter, Rusty got himself transferred to the Division band, where he played a clarinet for the duration. I'm sure he was grateful for my errant handling of the flame thrower.

I later proved that my aim with the M-1 rifle was no better than it had been with the flame-thrower. We were practicing how to take prisoners and my turn came to escort a "prisoner" role-played by one of our non-coms. When my prisoner failed to obey my orders, I shouted "halten Sie," and when he continued straight ahead I fired a shot over his head. It was just a blank round but it came close enough to his noggin to ring his bell, and I became subject to some unkind remarks.

My low-grade physical coordination skills capped my promotion potential early in my army career. An example of my physical ineptitude occurred when there was an opening to move up created by some of our older (19-year-old) comrades volunteering for combat duty. (These lads figured that nothing could be worse than infantry training in the swamps of Louisiana.) Joe Heitman and I competed to see who could set up the mortar faster. Joe was no track star, but he beat me handily, and I remained an assistant gunner until our squad leader was wounded in combat and replaced by Joe, which moved me up to the position of gunner. Joe got sergeant stripes and I remained a terminal Private first class.

During my free time in Louisiana and California I enjoyed listening to classical music records in USO clubs and music store booths and playing chess and contract bridge with friends who shared these interests, especially Steve Jarvis, Paul Mallon and Frank Kirchoff. Chess and bridge proved great time-killers on our extended cruises back and forth across both oceans.

Soon after extended maneuvers in the Louisiana outback, where I saw unimaginable poverty in share cropping communities with quaint names such as Dry Prong, I was called to the orderly Room to receive some bad news. Dad was seriously ill and I was given an emergency furlough to go home. I got there several days before Dad died, and I was able to be with him at night, which enabled Mother to get some much-needed rest. Shortly before he died, Dad asked me to always take good care of Mother.

The funeral was held in the front parlor, which had been my bedroom before I went into the army. This residential setting was common practice in those days. Some persons commented that I showed no outward signs of my grief, which was true, as I disliked displays of emotion on such occasions. After the funeral I requested a few days extension of my furlough so that I could help Mother with final arrangements, but my request was turned down.

Shortly after my return to Camp Livingston, the Division packed up and moved to Camp San Luis Obispo. After some arduous amphibious training run by Marines in Camp Pendleton, I was able to visit San Francisco with five buddies. We enjoyed the operetta Pirates of Penzance at the opera house and at the other end of the cultural scale a performance of Spike Jones and his City Slickers.

Soon after this pleasant outing, we were put on alert for a move overseas. We all expected to be put on ships bound for the Pacific Theatre. This logical assumption was deleted from the latrine rumor chart when we suddenly were issued cold weather woolen clothing in preparation for a train ride across country to Boston and hence to the European Theatre. We later learned that our Division was desperately needed to replace the thousands of troops lost in the German counter-offensive known as Battle of the Bulge in the Ardennes.

On February 19, 1945, the same day that our forces landed on Iwo Jima, we left Boston harbor aboard the former luxury liner Kungsholm, sister ship of the

Swedish America Lines Gripsholm, which had been used to exchange American and Japanese diplomats. With nearly 5,000 troops of the 342nd Infantry Regiment stuffed into a vessel designed for 1,000 passengers, this was no pleasure cruise. Zigzagging to avoid German U-boats our convoy took two weeks to cross the storm-tossed Atlantic. "K" Company was lodged on "E" (the lowest) deck aft. One evening "Red" Goodrich appeared on deck and said that he badly needed a breath of fresh air. I asked if he had gotten seasick. He related how there had been a chain reaction of comrades puking into their helmets down below. That wasn't too bad, he said, but he'd lost it when a little stowed-away puppy dog came along and started to lap up the vomit.

The night before we pulled into the bomb-scarred harbor of Le Havre, our destroyer escorts fired off dozens of depth charges to destroy enemy U-boats lurking in the waters below. The sweating steel bulkheads shook and emitted a deep, clanging sound as if the J. Arthur Rank gong-beater stood outside with is long-handled hammer trying to get our attention for the feature film. We figured the odds were against us being able to move up five decks to escape being trapped like rats if a torpedo should hit our ship. But we wanted to avoid a panic situation, so we moved at a deliberate pace. On arriving at the latrine on "A" deck, we almost wish we had stayed below. The air was filled with tobacco smoke (smoking on deck was strictly prohibited) mixed with the stench of ankle-deep waves of vomit and urine that rolled and pitched with ship's movements.

Our first stop on French soil was a tent city staging area in Normandy called Camp Lucky Strike. We cleaned our weapons, got our heads shaved and did our best to keep from freezing to death in tens warmed only when we were able to supplement our meager coal ration by scrounging bits of firewood from the local mayor's garden. I began to understand why the Normans had left this windswept countryside for England!

On March 22nd, we left Yvetot on the same 40 &8 boxcars that had been used by our troops in the first world war. After passing Liege, Belgium, and Maastricht, Holland, we reached the German border at Aachen, and continued by truck to a western suburb of the majestic cathedral city of Cologne. Here we were billeted in neat little bungalows tht smelled from backyard gardens fertilized by human waste compost. Red showed me a framed needlework poem that hung on a child's bedroom wall. He said that it was a bedtime prayer that his mother had taught him. I immediately recognized the German verse from my own childhood. *Ich bin klein, mein hertz ist rein* (I am small, my heart is clean), *soll nieman dritt wohnen als Jesu allein* (so no one will live there but Jesus along). Red just shook his head and muttered something about it being a small world turned upside down by the lunacy of war. I nodded.

We came within range of enemy guns for the first time a few days later when we relieved troops of the 8th Division on the western banks of the Rhine and took over their positions. During daylight hours we stayed in rooms in a tall apartment house. We were warned to say away from rooms on the east side with a view of the river and the Cathedral lest we become targets of 88 mm anti-tank guns mounted on river barges. Some of our comrades went up to these rooms anyway to get a good look at the river, and shortly after they returned downstairs 88 shells tore aware most of the top floor.

Each night after dark we moved into earthen bunkers overlooking the river looking for German patrols. *I've been told that we came under artillery fire, but I don't remember it.* (Italics added by editor) I later asked Red what he recalled about our nocturnal watch on the Rhine. He remembered the blood-chilling scream of the high velocity 88 shells that every so often flew overhead. I never heard them.

Some days later when we were deployed with the First Army in the battle of the Ruhr Pocket, we were taking a break on a wooded hillside when I fell asleep. Our company commander, Capt. Bruce MacAlister, looked down and saw me and asked "Is that man dead?" I have to admit that I had a real knack for sleeping whenever the opportunity arose. Maybe saying my prayers helped me to relax to the point of falling into a deep sleep almost instantaneously. Anyway, after my nap, we pushed on and took up positions on a wooded hillside. We were told to dig in as there would be an artillery barrage aimed at the town of Hilchenbach down in the valley below us. At my location there were so many tree roots and rocks that I gave up trying to dig a hole, and was leftr to hope that if there were tree bursts overhead, they not be right over my head. After the barrage, we occupied the town without any resistance that I can remember.

Some of my platoon mates recalled Hilchenbach rather differently. Austin "Red" Goodrich wrote the following about Hilchenbach, in his memoirs, *Born To Spy.*

"…Gradually the shells, including heavy stuff from Corps artillery batteries, came closer to the tops of the tall pines until there was only a split second interval between the whistle and the explosion. And then no interval at all. We were under the worst kind of friendly fire: tree bursts that spewed down jagged shards of steel in huge arcs of destruction. It was time to dig a hole to hide in, with an entrenching tool if you happened to have one (most of them had long since been ditched along with the cumbersome gas masks that had been the first excess baggage to go) or with your fingernails.

Nobody was standing or sitting. I shrunk into a fetal position at the base of a tree that I must have thought would shield at least part of me from the agents of death dispatched by our own artillery, whose topo lmaps failed to take into account the height of the trees on that hillside and were falling short. I pawed at the ground, sending pine needles flying until the explosions overhead got so intense that individual bursts meerged into a single ear-splitting roll of deadly thunder. Fear gave way to a numbed unity of mind and body. And I heard myself pray out loud: Please God, make 'em stop. Please...."

Red's assistant gunner, Steve Jarvis, remembered: *If Hilchenbach was where we took heavy shelling from our own artillery, where [Pfc] Kimball died crying in that black, appalling din, I was there and remember it all too clearly.*

My assistant gunner, Lloyd "Doc" Iverson wrote me: *I remember the time we were positioned on a hill and the artillery was shelling overhead. It was horrible. One of our riflemen called out for his mother.*

During the night, my sleep was interrupted by German troops marching by our house, which served as the K Company command post, as they pulled out of town. In a few hours I was to become a prisoner of these *soldaten.* The night was cold, pitch dark and silent except for the occasional rattle of German 20 mm antiaircraft canon mounted on half-tracks that fired at any sound or light from an American position. The silence was also shattered by a burst of a dozen .45 caliber rounds from Bob Guernsey's M-3 "grease gun," which pockmarked the vestibule walls and ceiling but only knocked the cap off the German soldier who had entered our front door without an invitation.

The next morning (April 11, 1945) before breakfast about a dozen of us were detailed as a patrol to go back up into the hills with a medic to attend t our dead and wounded comrades left behind. The point of our diamond formation had just about reached the line of trees when German troops of the crack Panzer Lehr Division stood up and demanded our surrender. Our sergeant saw that they had the drop on us and ordered us to drop our weapons.

One of our captors searched us and confiscated our invasion Marks, saying that "Der Fuehrer does not recognize this as money." I had only $10 worth at most. (I don't think I was ever reimbursed for my loss.) One of the first questions our captors asked was whether there were any Jews in our patrol. None admitted that there were any Jews in our group, which there were. At one point, the Germans discussed whether to kill us. I can still hear their voices: *Wir mussen zu Hagen gehen, unser Hauptkvartier.* (We must get to our headquarters at Hagen.) *Also, mussen wir gefangener schiessen so das wir einem besser faeltigkeit haven zurech zu gehen.* (Therefore, we must shoot the prisoners so that we have a better chance to get back.) Fortunately for us, this perfectly sound reasoning did not prevail.

By mid-afternoon, I was either talking to the others or possibly taking a nap. I was then called over to where a group of Americans and Germans were talking. I believe that Millimet and Kohlman wee trying to help translate. However their Yiddish wasn't quite doing the job. (Fortunately, their captors failed to recognize this as a Jewish tongue!) Eventually, the Germans surrendered to us after destroying their personal weapons so that we could not use them against their comrades who were still fighting.

For my brief stint as a POW, I was put in for a Bronze Star award with this supporting document: "Pfc John E. List without regard to his own safety volunteered to leave the town and go into the forest to evacuate some of his wounded comrades. In spite of the fact that enemy opposition was still heavy, he left with several others on their mission of mercy. While en route, the group was exposed several times and were fired upon by snipers. Near the completion of their mission, while attempting to cross an open field where the injured men lay, the patrol was pinned down by enemy machine gun fire, and being unable to move either forward or to the rear, were subsequently captured and held prisoner by the Germans until elements of the 99th Infantry Division came to thneir aid and captured their captors.

For his participation in this heroic attempt, above and beyond the call of duty, the Bronze Star is recommended.../signed/Robert E. Kohn, 1st Lt., 342nd Infantry, Commanding.

In Letter Orders dated 23 January 1952, when I was serving as a First Lt. at Fort Mason, I was finally awarded the medal "for exemplary conduct in ground combat on or about 11 April 1945 in the European Theater of Operations." Later President Eisenhower awarded the Bronze Star to all Blackhawk soldiers who had received the Combat Infantry Badge and served in the action at Berglern (April 30, 1945). So I guess my Bronze Star should bear an oak leaf cluster.

My sketchy memory of my capture in the area of Hilchenbach/Altenhunden and my inability to recall any of the combat in Berglern suggest that in both instances I must have suffered a form of temporary amnesia, which is now officially recognized as a symptom of post-traumatic stress disorder. (See end of chapter observations on this illness, its proven role in criminal behavior and how the court dismissed its relevancy in my trial.)

After several battles against dispirited Wehrmacht troops, who were often forced into fighting by fanatical Waffen SS units, the Blackhawks helped split the German forces in a south to north pincer movement through the Ruhr Valley.

We then left the 1st Army command and raced southeast through Bavaria under the command of Gen. George Patton's 3rd Army. We hated Patton simply because his racehorse tactics never gave us time to satisfy our overriding needs: Sleep, a shower, some clean clothes and a hot meal. On the other hand, many of us had to grudgingly admit later on that uncomfortable as it was, the speed of Patton's advance saved many of our lives. On several occasions, we surprised German troops who had no idea where we were coming from.

This was not the case, unfortunately, at Ingolstadt, where the enemy forces were dug in and prepared with the support of artillery and armor to repel any attempt to cross the Danube River. At the end of a long march and fire fights along the way, we longed for a night's rest in the high-rise apartment houses a few hundred yards back from the banks of the brown-not-blue Danube. Instead the order was passed down to get ready to cross. It was said that Gen. Patton himself had issued the order to mount an amphibious assault across the river as soon as possible. (As if that would make us feel any better about the operation!)

Combat Engineers hastily dumped loads of 10-man plywood skiffs a few hundred yards short of the river's edge and took off to the rear in a cloud of dust pierced by screaming 88 artillery shells. I never saw trucks move that fast, before or since. Red told me how he was hunkered down in a foxhole next to a demolished bridge, his hearing impaired by 88 shells flying a few feet over head. Suddenly something metallic struck his helmet and he thought he had bought the farm, only to discover that he'd been struck by a .50 cal. Machine gun shell casing dropped from a P-47 strafing a shack (maybe a German artillery observation post) across the river.

I don't remember how we got across, only that K Company of the 342nd Infantry were the first troops to cross the Danube River, despite claims by other units, including the engineers(!), that they were first. I was told later that our exec, Lt. "Red" Brown was killed in the crossing. In his unpublished memoirs, my squad leader Joe Heitman, deceased, wrote: *I don't know how any of us lived through the night. We were moving across the River Styx and Cerberus waited on the other side.*

It was indescribably awful, Joe wrote, *shells wee bursting all over and machine gun fire was lacing back and forth in the water. I took a few good looks around, very few, and spent the rest of the trip with my head down looking at the back of the man in front of me. That damned awkward bathtub of a skiff had all the speed of an overladen garbage scow. Finally, after what seemed like several centuries, we arrived at the far shore along with one other skiff filled with men of the weapons platoon. About 70 men from Co. K held the bridgehead of about 75 yards deep from 2145 to 2300 hours, when I Co got across. Units that followed, without benefit of artillery covering fire, which had to be stopped to avoid hitting our own troops on the enemy shore, took a terrible beating. Several boats suffered direct hits from German mortars. The second platoon lost 24 of its 42 men.*

After we got across the river, we dug slit trenches. A deeper fox hole would have filled with water. Even the slit trench was damp. There was a barn several hundred yards ahead of us. Some of the men went there and brought back straw, which we put into our trenches. This helped to keep the trench more comfortable.

Having had a busy day, I soon fell asleep. Joe came over to wake me up several times as I was snoring very loudly. He was concerned that the Germans would hear me and attack. I later read that we were a very thin line holding the bridgehead, and our mortars were part off this ragged line. I don't remember much of that night, however, perhaps because I fell asleep when I was supposed to be awake and on guard. It is difficult to remain awake when one is lying down in a shallow trench. It is much easier to stay awake when one is walking a guard post. (Goodrich comment: *It seems incredible to me that List was able to sleep that night, what with the sounds of artillery over head and the need to stay alert to to guard our thin line against an expected German counter attack. It was so dark that we had to challenge for a password whenever any shadowy human movement was detected. One such movement turned out to be the company commander of L Company, whom I almost shot before he identified himself. He was looking for any member of his company. Apparently they were dispersed along the river bank in such a scattered way, that their commander couldn't locate a single one of them! Sleep on that night? No way.*)

A few days later, I recalled that it was early morning when we crossed the [Isar Mittel] canal. The main bridge had been blown before we arrived. The footbridge no doubt was intended to be a good "killing zone" for the defenders. We did received c some incoming artillery or mortar fire after crossing the bridge. We briefly hit the dirt. Captain "Mac" [Macalister] came by and got us moving. I remember running into the town of Berglern on a well-used path. A German soldier ws wounded and laying across the path. I could tell that he was afraid that we might jump on him. I jumped over him. The man was dead, according to Heitman, who wrote to me: "I think you never saw any dead soldiers because you didn't want to see them."

The next thing I remember it was about 5:00 p.m.. (Goodrich Comment: Apparently List blacked out during at least seven hours of the heaviest combat experienced by K Co, 342nd Infantry Regiment. In *ex post facto* recognition of this battle, President Eisenhower later awarded the Bronze Star medal for valor to all of the men who were engaged in this full day of fighting. Although List could not recall firing his 60 mm mortar, his squad leader, Heitman, reported that List fired all of the 40 rounds available to him on that day. This would seem to be proof positive that Pfc John List suffered a total lapse of memory, which is a hallmark symptom of post traumatic stress disorder, with which List has been diagnosed and is receiving in prison from the Veterans Administration 10 per cent disability compensation.)

We were in a typical farm courtyard, I was at the mortar overlooking an open field, sound asleep. Apparently I was supposed to be on guard. Joe [squad leader Joseph Heitman] came by, woke me up and let me know that one could be executed for falling asleep on guard duty at the front.

That was the day that Capt. Mac [K Co. Commander Bruce Macalister, who received the Silver Star posthumously] was killed and I heard that some of our riflemen refused to take any more prisoners that day, shooting some who had their hands raised attempting to give up.

After we got back to the States, I often wondered why we were sent to Europe, since we didn't get into any real fighting. [!] For the same reason I couldn't understand why we had all been awarded the Combat Infantry Badge. Years later, after I'd read *Blackhawks Over the Danube* (by Richard Briggs, Western Recorder, Louisville, KY, 1954) in 1990, which recounts all of the action that K Company was in, I realized that we had engaged in our fair share of combat. My squad leader, Joe Heitman, documented in detail some of the fighting that we had. Joe mentioned that in the fighting at Berglern, for which we were later awarded the Bronze Star, our mortar squad fired all of its 40 rounds. Joe also remembered how he had fired his M-1 carbine until he had run out of ammo. To this day I don't remember those actions, or that my assistant gunner, "Doc" Iverson, had dropped a single shell into the tube of my 60 mm mortar.

In a letter that reached me in prison, dated May 15, 1994, Joe Heitman (deceased) my squad leader, (later an attorney in Tacoma, Washington) who was never separated from me during the war except for the day when I was captured, wrote: "I always had you figured for having iron nerves in combat. Maybe it was an outward manifestation of any attempt to forget what was going on—hence your lack of memory....Memories are strange things. Very often stressful times are quickly forgotten. Some actions in Germany were quickly forgotten and some I remember as if it were yesterday. You may recall that I had an experience with PTSD in the Philippines. It took the form of stomach ulcers. The doctor at the base hospital diagnosed it as the result of a stressful period in Europe followed by garrison idleness in the Pacific. He advised me to ask for extra and stressful duty which I did and which cured the ulcers."

More than half a century after the war, on several occasions in my prison cell I experienced a fuzzy sort of day dream. In it, I ride in an uncovered two and a half ton Army truck, which in drizzling rain and darkness passes through German lines to the outskirts of the medieval city of Ludenscheid in the Ruhr Valley.

My squad leader remembered details of the Ludenscheid operation, which somehow were blacked out in my memory, including how war could sometimes produce a sort of twisted comedy. Joe wrote:

"Moving into the main square of Ludenscheid, our 2nd Mortar Squad followed behind the Second Platoon. After a block or so, the platoon was stopped behind a pile of rubble by heavy fire from behind a similar pile about a black ahead. The Krauts blocking our advance were old pros and the firefight became hot and heavy. After several minutes of this, I went up to direct mortar fire and crouched down behind the barricade. Suddenly, a door flew open in a building next to the German position and a man in a business suit carrying a briefcase walked out into the middle of the street. He smiled, waved his briefcase over his head and yelled in German, "Don't shoot! I'm a civilian, and I have to get to work." The whole firefight stopped, while soldiers on both sides shouted at the civilian. "Get outta here you dumb Kraut! *Raus, Du Hanswurst, Verflugter Zivilist!*" All the time this screaming was going on, the civilian cheerfully waved his brief case, admonished us not to shoot and walked toward our barricades. Finally he reached us and turned into a narrow street to our right. We dogfaces and our Lanser enemies then resumed the battle. (War is truly madness!) We then dispersed out adversaries with mortar fire."

I must have been manning the mortar, but I have no recollection whatsoever of this close combat encounter in downtown Ludenscheid.

I have no explanation for my combat amnesia. Of course, I remembered the time of my capture, something of crossing the Danube and some of the fighting in Ludenscheid. And that's about it. It is strange that some who have been in combat keep reliving their experience. I, on the other hand, can't remember, even when details are told to me. Perhaps my old friend, Patrick H. Daoust, MD, of Dearborn, MI shed some clinical light on my condition in a letter to me dated August 10, 1997:

"David Herold's 342nd Inf. Log mentions a day that sounds very much like the day you said you could remember only the beginning and end of during which you were told you fired over 40 mortar rounds to break up a German attack [at Berglern]. It sounds to me to be a clear-cut case of amnesia. This kind of amnesia would only result from extreme mental trauma. In your case it would occur in a person who was basically very strong but who at the same time possessed a very gentle nature. Thus, your actions on that day would have run very counter to that gentle nature, which not surprisingly would produce amnesia. This would account for the fact that not only on that day, but at other times during your involvement in combat situations, you had no recollection of your experiences. Your memory of these situations simply produced a blank screen. I believe very strongly that it's highly likely that you did suffer from Post-Traumatic Stress Disorder and that this very well could have influenced your subsequent behavior."

Recent research of PTSD by the Veterans' Administration's National Center for PTSD and others has shown that the illness is much more prevalent than was thought when it was first proposed as a diagnosis in 1980. Moreover, it has been found that for some WWII veterans, war trauma memories a half century after the war continue to cause severe problems. Inability to recall traumatic experiences in combat (disassociation and psychogenic amnesia) is accepted as one of the six symptoms of the disorder. The so-called avoidance/numbing criterion appears in PTSD as a sort of defense mechanism to cut off the conscious experience of trauma-based memories and feelings.

An overview by Dr. Matthew J. Friedman published by the VA National Center for PTSD in 2000 concludes that "psychic numbing" is an emotional anesthesia that makes it extremely difficult for people with PTSD to participate in meaningful interpersonal relationships.

A *Fact Shee*t published by the National Center for PTSD dated May 16m 2000 contains a more specific finding: "Trauma survivors with PTSD often experience problems in their intimate and family relationships or close friendships. PTSD involves symptoms that interfere with trust, emotional closeness, communication, responsible assertiveness, and *effective problem solving*. [My italics] The possibility that PTSD suffered in combat during the war might have influenced the action that led to the murders at my hand of my immediate family was never introduced during my trial. Dr. Sheldon Miller, a psychiatrist, made a strong case that I suffered from a major depressive disorder when I killed my family, but Judge William L'Estrange Wertheimer, (sometimes referred to as "Willie the Weird") would have none of it. Instead, the magistrate used my diagnosed *compulsive-obsessive disorder* as reason for imposing the maximum sentence of five consecutive life terms on the grounds that this disorder would increase the chance of my repeating the murders if I were ever released. The relevancy of post-traumatic stress disorder as a mitigating factor was ruled out in my post conviction relief (PCR) appeal. Moreover, none of my Army comrades, whose names and addresses I had provided to my PCR public defender, Ms. Pamela A. Brause, was ever contacted to provide information pertaining to my combat experience in World War II or to testify at my Post Conviction Relief (PCR) Hearing.

In rejecting my petition for PCR as being "patently without merit," Judge Wertheimer, who had presided at my original trial averred that my claim regarding PTSD only made matters worse for my case. He opined: "Now defendant comes before this Court and makes some general and generic references that his dastardly deeds are excusable by virtue of undiagnosed and untreated post traumatic stress disorder. By doing that, he demonstrates lack of remorse for his admitted acts….By doing that he offends all those who really do suffer from post-traumatic stress disorder, but that is easy for defendant to do, because we know he is a man without honor."

Ironically, the absence of my conscious recall of combat stress, itself a hallmark symptom of the disorder, is cited by the magistrate as cause to dismiss its relevancy. In his words:

"Defendant's psychiatrist submitted a fourteen-page report which revealed a thorough examination of the defendant. His entire life was researched and his military service was detailed without the slightest hint of any psychological or psychiatric problems while in the service or any sequelae attributable to the service. Defendant's clinical psychologist spent one sentence, fourteen words on defendant's military history. That is how significant he felt it to be, and he concluded, 'There is no question that Mr. List knew what was happening.'

"It is, therefore incredible that defendant would attempt to raise the specter of post-traumatic stress disorder….While the suggestion that he suffered from post traumatic stress disorder at the time of these murders may now seem incredible, it is predictable for this man without honor….Neither his psychiatrist nor his psychologist believed he suffered from such a disorder at the time of the events. If he does suffer it now, its etiology is more likely the result of his actions on November 9, 1071, than anything else."

As a jurist, Wertheimer must have known this statement to be pure speculation without any scientific foundation. Moreover, his specious disregard for the relevance of PTSD in my case was contradicted in writing by a scientific finding published in a New Jersey State Prison-Main Chart Document dated May 17, 2001, signed by a psychiatrist, a psychologist and a social worker. This official finding states: "Inmate [myself] has PTSD as evidenced by subjective feelings of distress re his war experiences. Treatment goal set for May 15, 2002: Inmate will experience reduced symptoms of PTSD such that he can function with minimal problems in the GP [General Population] environment."

It is clear from this finding that I must have suffered from post-traumatic stress disorder at the time of my murderous rampage (at a point halfway between my combat experience and my official diagnosis of PTSD) and that this should have been considered by the court as a mitigating factor and/or evidence of ineffective counsel. Instead, PTSD was overlooked both in my trial and in my appeals, including, my petition for post conviction relief (PCR). At no time did my PCR counsel see fit to make contact by mail, telephone or FAX with any of my Army comrades, including Joe Heitman and "Red" Goodrich, whose names and addresses were supplied by me to the Public Defenders Office in a timely fashion. Thus, the first-hand knowledge and testimony of these Army witnesses never had a chance to be heard.

At the risk of boring the reader by beating a dead horse, let me reference a Fact Sheet published by the National Center for PTSD dated march 20, 2002. In this study, researchers Claudia Baker and Cessie Alfonso cite cases of capital crimes in which defendants suffering from PTSD were found not guilty by reason of insanity, one of them on appeal of his conviction. The study concludes that, contrary to what happened in my case, "The presence of PTSD is a factor that should be considered by the court during sentencing. If a defendant is diagnosed with PTSD, this information should be introduced as a mitigating factor during the penalty phase of a capital case. In states with versions of the "three strikes" law and in federal cases, the presence of PTSD may be reason for the court to depart from mandatory sentencing guidelines."

If in my case the court erred in its failure to consider my PTSD, it was equally culpable of twisting the effect of my other personality problem—my compulsive/obsessive personality disorder—in regard to the imposition of a consecutive terms sentence. Judge Wertheimer supported his decision to impose the maximum sentence of five consecutive life terms by misconstruing the effect of my diagnosed compulsive-obsessive personality disorder. Here are his words, which I find most troubling: *We know from this trial that he [List] still suffers from a compulsive-obsessive personality disorder, which his expert claimed triggered these events. Thus, if he ever returns to the community, there is a real risk that he could reprise these horrific acts, and that is not a risk this court is willing to assume."*

First, my experts never claimed that this disorder (a personality trait shared by most accountants) triggered my killing, though I can see how it may have influenced the orderly manner in which I went about my terrible actions. More important, so long as this disorder persists, is there reason to believe that the person so afflicted will be more inclined than others to repeat a violent crime? Although Dr. Simring has declined to comment on this question, other psychologists I have contacted for an opinion have, albeit off the record, described Judge Wertheimer's conclusion as "patently absurd."

Although World War II set the stage for only 30 months of my life, including just 41 days of combat, it may have had a pivotal effect on my personality and behavior. Let's take a brief look at the events and the people with whom I shared my life in the 86th Blackhawk Division.

According to its official history, the 86th Division in World War II:

1. Was the first Allied Division to cross the Danube River;

2. Captured 53,354 German prisoners;

3. Liberated more than 200,000 Allied prisoners of war;

4. Conquered 220 miles of German territory;

5. Captured the Hungarian Crown Jewels;

6. Made amphibious assaults across the Danube, Bigge, Altmuhl, Isar, Inn and Salzach rivers, and the Amper and Mittel Isar canals;

7. Served in combat with four different U. S. Armies in the European Theatre (the 1st, 3rd, 7th and 15th a record for the western front.

8. Was one of only two divisions to serve in both the European and Pacific Theatres of Operation (the other was the 97th Division.)

My 86th Division, 342nd Infantry Regiment comrades in arms remember:

Squad leader Joe Heitman (deceased):

Our entry into Austria marked the last day of the war. In retrospect, I wonder that anyone in K Co. got out alive…At the very least, we should thank John for being a good soldier.

Bob Guernsey, K Co. Mortar Squad mate:

I don't remember any notable events involving John. I thought he was a good soldier and friend. I don't understand the tragedy many years later that engulfed him and those connected to him. I feel sorry for John, but I feel sorrier for those who suffered because of him.

Lloyd "Doc" Iverson, Mortar Squad mate:

The only thing I remember about John is that he was very much a loner, attended church quite faithfully, and I thought conscientious about his duties as a soldier.

Walt "Rusty" Hayes, Mortar Squad mate:

I remember John as being quiet, meek, studious and the last person you'd ever expect violence from. I retain a mental image of him as tall and lanky, with glasses being a dominant feature along with an oversized helmet that always looked in danger of falling off.

Steve Jarvis, 4th Platoon mate:

John and I were especially good friends in K Col, sharing a love of classical music, and generally being very compatible personalities. We spent many hours together in camp and in town, especially in St. Louis Obispo, CA, at the library and in the booths of music stores listening to classical music records. I think John and I were attracted to each other because we both had rather introverted personalities. We got along quite well, perhaps boring each other, but liking each other despite our absolutely opposing philosophical, religious and political views.

When John disappeared, I sincerely hoped he was a suicide. I can understand, in a manner of speaking, what life must have been like for him: a demented wife torturing him constantly, a very unsympathetic mother to his children, and as a result children who probably gave him no respect, and were no doubt rebellious. Yet his sense of duty to his family and his religious beliefs precluded his running away or committing suicide, which I would probably have done. Instead, he had an emotional breakdown which must have turned him into another person. There's no doubt about the extensive premeditation in the crime, which does not at all square with the John of before or since.

Paul Mallon K Co comrade:

I thought John to be highly intelligent but rather introverted and when after the war I heard that he had become an accountant, I thought it an appropriate niche for his type of personality. I find it hard to believe, however, that he could remember no combat situations in Germany. Ours was certainly not a "D Day" epic, but there were situations both in the Ruhr and afterwards when we were under hostile fire and taking casualties and I, for one, felt it very much a real war.

My post-war contacts with John occurred in the mid-60's when he accepted a position with a Jersey City bank as comptroller and we got together periodically for luncheon and gossip. Towards the end of the [60's] decade (when he was selling life insurance) he seemed in good spirits and happy. I had several more meetings with him and learned that he was experiencing difficulties in sales and feeling financial pressures. The news of his rampage in late 1971 came like a bombshell and I found it hard to believe. He did not seem the type and I became convinced that he must have experienced some sort of mental breakdown.

Austin "Red" Goodrich, Platoon mate:

John List came across as the most gentle soul I had ever known. He smiled a lot, was soft-spoken, never swore or told dirty jokes and was kind to everyone. He was built like a pear and always appeared to be on the verge of tripping over his own feet. All of which made one feel a little sorry for this church-going scholar being immersed in the dirty-minded, rough and tumble life of the infantry. He just didn't fit in the Army mold. Only later did I come to admire his intellect and feel compassion for his tragic inability to cope with the harsh realities of an ungentle world.

3

Graduation, Re-up and Romance

It was a real thrill to get back home after thirty months in the Army, including seven months of garrison duty in tent camps on Luzon and Mindanao in the Philippines. The war officially ended while we were on board a troop ship on our way to the Pacific Theatre. We had been slated to participate in the invasion of the main island of Japan. The A-bomb changed that plan, which saved a million lives including, very possibly, my own. There were no "ban-the-bomb" supporters to be found among the Blackhawks.

By and large our service in the Philippines was extended boredom interspersed with swatting at softballs and insects. To protect against malaria spread by mosquitos we were ordered to take a little yellow Atabrine pill every day. If you followed this order your skin acquired a yellowish hue and it was rumored that the pill didn't prevent the disease anyway but only suppressed its symptoms. Most of the pills were tossed into drainage ditches, leaving people who followed orders like me easily identified by their lemony complexion.

One of our main jobs was to dig drainage ditches, which we promptly subbed out to scrawny little Japanese POW's. In contrast to the ditches we dug, which snaked between our tents in irregular paths at varying depths, the little 80 lb POW's used a borrowed piece of string and wooden stakes to lay out perfectly straight trenches dug at precise and uniform depths. I recall how energetic and regimented our prisoners were. They worked from dawn to dusk and only took a break when we ordered them to do so.

In this same vein, our slave labor prisoners demonstrated an ingrained sense of discipline and respect for authority that was conspicuously lacking among the civilians in uniform who won the war that the losers had started. For example, whenever we tried to give one of them a cigarette, he would smile, bow deeply and point to his sergeant. We finally understood that all benefits had to be channeled through the chain of command. The sergeant would take the proffered cigarettes and ration them out to his charges, sometimes dividing them in two to save the butts for later distribution.

I was also struck by how these people who had demonstrated such arrogance and bestial behavior when they were on top (recalling the rape of Nanking and the Baatan Death March, which had been brought home to me most vividly by photos in Life magazine), could be so servile, even obsequious as losers.

In any case, I had to admire their excellent taste in food. They all politely declined the C and K rations we offered them in favor of retrieving food from the garbage cans that held the uneaten portions of our mess hall's *haute cuisine*.

Our extended presence in the Philippines may have had less to do with military need (capturing Japanese diehard outposts and denying the acquisition of weapons by the nascent communist guerillas in the jungles of Mindanao) than with the need to forestall a major depression that economists predicted would happen if 15 million servicemen were dumped onto an economy geared to wartime production. In any case, we were more than a little eager to get home and get on with our lives.

I was told that our Division's Commander, General Melasky (aka "beet nose") had received a letter from my mother requesting him to please bring his troops home as soon as possible. I have no doubt that Mother wrote such a letter. Her desire for the return of her only child was doubtless sharpened by her having lost her husband, my Dad, a year before we got to the Philippines.

Apparently this letter had as little effect as letters to the editor of the armed forces newspaper, Stars and Stripes, which complained about the unequal application of the points system, which was used to determine eligibility for discharge. A rather complex formula, including factors such as marital status, length of service and time spent in combat theatres, determined the order of qualifying for the "ruptured duck," an honorable discharge pin. We were upset by letters from home that told us of how some of our peers with fewer points than we had been discharged. When some of our complaints were published, members of the Blackhawk Division were held up to ridicule as "Squawkhawks." When our battalion commander, Maj. Ward, heard that this derogatory term had been used by non-combat troops, he assured everyone in his command that an appropriate physical reaction to anyone who voiced the offensive label would never be punished.

The trip back across the Pacific was shorter and more pleasant than the east-to-west voyage had been. For one thing, the troop transports' lights were turned on. I'll never forget one enchanted evening, when I sat down on the deck in an open passageway to listen to an impromptu piano concert. I have no idea how a piano got on a troop transport, but the beautiful rendition of Beethoven's Moonlight Sonata performed by a concert pianist dressed in rumpled green fatigues is a scene I shall never forget. I guess it was just one of those little incongruities that occasionally enrich our lives.

It felt good to get back to Bay City, to get dressed in civies and to be reunited with family and classmates. I remember that two were conspicuously absent: Zion Church member Warren Schramm, and Donald Hetzner, both of whom had been a year older than I, both killed in action.

Like most survivors, I promptly enrolled in the 52-20 Club, which provided veterans with a government unemployment check of $20 for up to 52 weeks. I also signed up for a class in shorthand at the Bay City Business School. I figured this skill would serve me well for taking notes when I got to the University of Michigan. I dropped out of the course, however, when I realized about halfway through that I would never be fast enough for the skill to be of any use to me in college.

After a few weeks, I renewed my friendship with Pat Doust and we visited Ann Arbor to find out about enrolling in the U of M for study under the G.I. Bill, an enlightened post WW II law that gave veterans enough money to pay for their room and board and covered the costs of books and class fees. Michigan was taking all returning sons of the state who could meet entrance requirements. Enrollment doubled and skeptics feared that the postwar student population balloon would burst as soon as the tidal wave of vets subsided. It never did, and the high enrollment of the immediate postwar years persisted, to the long-term benefit of our country.

During the war, the Parker Pen Co. advertised its Parker 51 as the world's best pen, because the company was engaged in war work, consumers would have to wait until after the war to buy one. (That reminded me of the Lucky Strike cigarette ad that proclaimed "Lucky Strike Green has gone to War," to explain it change from green to white packaging, a move which I later learned had nothing to do with the war effort. The change was in response to a survey which revealed that Chesterfield cigarettes were winning the bigger share of the burgeoning female smokers market by packaging their lethal product in a "clean," white package favored by the fair sex.)

In any case, I couldn't wait to visit Ulrich's book and office supply store to buy a Parker 51. I wore my gold-colored honorable discharge pin and this must have impressed the clerk, probably a high school student, who addressed me as "Sir." That was the first time anyone had called me that, and it made me feel good, much older than my 21 years.

Like most vets, I couldn't wait to get through college and out into the real world. To this end, I attended summer schools and always signed up for two or three more credit hours than the standard 15 hours per semester. This left precious little time for social life, including dating, which was nearly ruled out anyway by the scarcity of co-eds. Males must have out-numbered females on the campus by at least ten to one in those days. Occasionally I had time and funds for a movie at the Strand and a few beers at Schwabens or The Old German, real sawdust-on-the-floor beer joints shunned by the BMOC frat crowd who populated the more trendy Pretzel Bell. Once in a while I accompanied a friend to the local American Legion post where delicious pickled pork hocks were kept in a large jar behind the bar.

I shared a room in the West Quadrangle with Earl Sommers, a high school friend from Bay City, and a pharmacy major vet, who was a cheerful man, despite his serious war wound. We slept three to a room, one in a double-deck bunk, and had to study in shifts at a double desk. In our large cafeteria dinning room I occasionally enjoyed a chat with Red Goodrich, who lived at the far end of the same college housing unit. Red later moved into the Psi Upsilon fraternity house. I never had enough time for or interest in joining any of the Greek societies.

I visited my home in Bay City about once a month, hitchhiking whenever weather permitted. I had no trouble getting rides, perhaps because I carried a laundry case with a large block "M" embossed on its side. It's a shame that hitchhiking has become obsolete, killed by insurance company liability regulations. I had many interesting conversations with drivers who gave me lifts, including one man who conducted opinion surveys for a U of M polling company on public expectations for the national economy.

Contrary to what has been written about my life after my murders, Mother only very rarely came to visit me in Ann Arbor. If that were the only error published in these unauthorized biographies, I wouldn't mind. (Of the more than eighty factual errors I have counted, there was one published book of so-called creative non-fiction that stated as fact that I had served during WWII in an Army medical unit!)

On Sundays I attended a Lutheran Chapel established in 1942 and affiliated with the Missouri Synod. On Sunday evenings, both in a remodeled house and later in a church building, there was a supper and a social hour when we played cards, mostly contract bridge.

My career plan to become a research chemist, based on my belief that this was the area of our industrial economy with the brightest future, fizzled in my junior year. I simply lacked the ability to get the high grades needed to get a masters degree and a doctorate, which I'd need to succeed in this career. My academic impasse arrived when I fell sound asleep while cramming for a final exam in Organic Chemistry with two pre-med students. A sleep-inducing anti-histamine I was taking for a severe case of hay fever may have been at least partly responsible for a sub-par performance that produced the worst grade that I ever received in college. Rather than quit, I switched.

The School of Business Administration and I were a better fit. I enjoyed the logic of accounting much more than the memorization of facts about how substances react to each other. And anyway, who wants to spend the rest of their life in a smelly lab?

What was to become another crucial milestone in my life occurred at about the same time: I signed up for military service in the Transportation Corps of the Reserve Officers Training Program (ROTC). After Yugoslavia shot down one of our aircraft a year of two earlier and we had meekly responded with a mere verbal protest, I became convinced that our demonstrated weakness would encourage a larger aggressor (theUSSR) to wage a war in which we would become involved sooner rather than later. I wanted to avoid at all costs being drafted to serve once again as an enlisted infantryman in the coming war. So I signed up for enlistment in the Transportation Corps, as far from the infantry as I could get I got my commission as a 2nd Lieutenant in the Reserves at the conclusion of a summer camp at Ft Eustis, VA. In retrospect, my WWII squad leader, Joe Heitman, may have been right when he wrote that I was motivated to return to the Army mainly by my desire to prove myself a success, a leader of men, evidenced by having a uniform adorned by the bars of a commissioned officer. If this is true, the same driving ambition to succeed may have been responsible for the diligence and hard work that enabled me to graduate from the U of M with enough credits for a master's degree in Business Administration in four years. I was also chosen for an internship with Ernst and Ernst, a leading accounting firm in Detroit.

I received my BA at a ceremony held in Michigan Stadium in June of 1950. Mother gave me a new Ford car as a graduation present. In early September I went to work for E&E and was able to rent a room from Pat Doust and his new wife, also named Pat, in a nice neighborhood in east Detroit. How lucky I was. My rent was low and Mrs. Pat even made breakfast for me. I studied like mad to pass the first part of the Certified Accounting exam, and everything was coming up roses when I received orders to serve my country in another war in a different way in a different place: Korea.

After taking leave from E&E, I joined Mr. and Mrs. Pat, as I called them, for a few days visit in Bay City. I spent Thanksgiving 1950 with Mother and that

Saturday on my way back into the Army I listened to the U of M football game on the radio. This was the day that every Michigan Wolverine football fan of that era recalls as the date of the "Snow Bowl," played on snow-covered Ohio Stadium in Columbus, where we upset the favored Buckeyes and our great left halfback, Chuck Ortmann, kicked 24 punts, most of them on first or second down.

A photo of that game was one of the sports memorabilia that adorned the walls of the men-only Michigan Union cafeteria where students used to gather to eat unhurried cafeteria meals at oaken tables indented with carved initials. At a visit years later, I was saddened to see that the photos had been removed and the tables replaced with antiseptic Formica in the style of MacDonalds. Progress? I don't think so.

On my drive to begin active duty in California, I got to appreciate the beauty of the west even more than I had during the troop train journey from Camp San Luis Obispo to Ft. Miles Standish in Massachusetts en route to combat some six years before.

I had been in Fort Mason before, en route to and from the Philippines. I learned shortly after checking in that I was listed as Absent Without Leave (AWOL). What a great start for my second go-around in the U.S. Army! Either I left Bay City on the date I was to report or I had taken longer than the allowed number of days for my travel. In either case, I was clearly tardy. Fortunately, the pretty young ladies at Personnel set things right by simply giving me some leave days. Voila! Rank has its privileges, even for a lowly second lieutenant.

I used my clothing allowance for uniforms, which I adorned with the service ribbons I had brought along for that purpose. There were not many others around there who had both European and Pacific Theatre campaign ribbons together with the Combat Infantryman's badge.

The diversity of our population was brought home to me when I quickly met people who could have passed as our recent blood enemies. Several Nisei Japanese Americans, who had been relocated to internment camps during the war, worked in my Controllers Department. They were pleasant fellows, entirely different than the POW's in the Philippines, and after we got to know each other, they paid me the honor of inviting me to join their bowling team. In San Francisco, I looked up Mother's brother, Otto List, who took me along to St.Paul's Lutheran Church. His two daughters had married German immigrants who were as nice as anyone you'd ever want to know. Only in America!

One day I was given the opportunity to transfer from Fiscal and Budget to the Personnel Department of the controllers Division. This was an offer I probably should have accepted, since it might have served to improve my people skills, but

I turned it down. Why was I unwilling to embark on what could have been a career- and possibly life-enhancing opportunity? I have to believe it was because I have always had a tendency to forge ahead on the path I'm on, driven by inertia and equipped with blinders that prevent my consideration of alternative courses.

Sometimes I reinforce my inertia by rationalizing the status quo as the best situation. For example, after two weeks of detached duty at Camp Stoneman to help with the basic training of inductees, I was sitting in the Officer's Club waiting to go back to Ft. Mason. Suddenly, a man arrived with three or four beautiful women in tow. He was a brother of Bob Crosby, the big band leader, and the women were part of his show scheduled to entertain the troops in a week or so. With a little, very little, encouragement, we began to dance with the showgirls. The little beauty I danced with invited me to come back when they put on their show. I didn't make a commitment one way or the other. I reasoned that probably there would be plenty of local officers to keep the ladies company, but if a relationship did develop it would be difficult to maintain, because either I might be sent overseas or she would be on another band gig. Was I engaging in flagrant overthink? Was I being overly cautious? Probably.

Later in the spring of 1951, I attended a Fiscal and Budget course at Fort Ben Harrison outside Indianapolis. While there, I drove up to Ann Arbor for a dance held by the BizAd school. My date was a young lady I had gone out with in Bay City and had corresponded with while in San Francisco. We met in Ann Arbor and stayed overnight—unfortunately in separate rooms—at the Michigan Union. After my school at Ben Harrison ended, I drove up to Bay Cit and had some more dates with the lady. It was not she who accompanied me on my drive out to San Francisco, however, but Mother, who had never seen the West and wanted to visit family members out there. We had a pleasant trip seeing all the tourist sights from the Upper Peninsula of Michigan to Salt Lake City, the Rockies, Reno and Donner Pass.

Mother was able to stay at a visitors' facility on the base, and we ate meals together at a nearby cafeteria. Mother enjoyed spending time with Otto's family, and shopping with his friend. She also contacted a nephew of Aunt Ida, who had lived in the Chicago area before getting a divorce and moving to San Francisco to live with another man. I was so naïve that at the time I didn't realize that theirs was gay relationship.

I received orders to attend Transportation School in Fort Eustis, Virginia, in early September, 1951. Mother and I got back in my car for the drive east, taking a more direct route than when we were sightseeing on the way out. We stayed at Mother's for a few days, and I had a date or two with my lady friend, before getting back into my Ford for the drive to Virginia via the new Pennsylvania Turn-pike, which cut straight through the mountains to cut several hours of driving time and road stress.

At Fort Eustis, I got my Bachelor Officer Quarters assignment and started classroom instruction with officers from all over the U.S. and a few from Korea. During after hours, I hung out with two WW II vets I'll call Bob Oregon and John Washington. We soon found out where we could buy liquor on the base and frequently had our own happy hour before going to supper.

One weekend, Bob and I went to a bowling alley with two other officers from Kansas who were not WW II vets. Soon after we got there, two attractive young ladies arrived and Bob struck up a conversation. He gave me the high sign to join in and we soon discovered that they were sisters. The brunette was a woman named Jean Syfert, wife of a lieutenant serving on TDY (temporary duty) at an air base on a remote island in the Pacific. Her sister, the one with the light brown hair, was named Helen Taylor. She was recently widowed when her late husband, Marvin Taylor, an infantry lieutenant was killed in action in Korea. She had a daughter, Brenda, about nine years old. Jean had thought it was time for her grieving sister to get out of the house for a while, and they had come to the bowling alley. Thus, the stage was set for what would be a tragedy.

Bob talked the women into going with us to a B.B.Q. drive-in. We drove and ate in separate cars, but we agreed to meet the following weekend at their home, where they lived with their mother, Eva Morris, a widow. We drove behind them to be sure that we'd know where they lived. That's how it started. Bob and I followed up by having several, but no double dating, with the ladies.

Helen showed me several historic sites in the area, including the battlefield at Yorktown and the Mariners Museum. On some Saturdays Jean and Helen drove to our BOQ to watch us wash our cars. On other dates we went to the Officers Club or to attend services at the base chapel.

For some time my sexual urges had been, belatedly, forcing themselves to the surface. These feelings had been kept in check by my conviction that I should avoid sex until marriage, which would have to await completion of college and achieving a career a notch or two above entry level. As an officer in the Army, I was now secure, on solid ground both financially and socially. This unlocked the rational gates to sexual expression at the same time as my religion-founded moral sanctions were overcome by urges that grew with the passage of time. I was a 26-year-old virgin for heaven's sake!

Somewhere I had read or heard that women who were widowed or divorced were more easily seduced because they were used to having sex frequently. In my situation at the time, that very thought agitated my natural yearnings well beyond the limits imposed by my strict religious upbringing. Helen and I had been necking for some time and enjoying it. After an evening at the officers' club where we both had plenty to drink, we went back to her apartment where we engaged in foreplay to the point where Helen indicated that, yes, she wanted some real sex. Gee, golly, I wouldn't mind. I'd been carrying condoms in my wallet for some time in hopes of putting them to use. We were soon making love, wonderful love. Or was it just carnal sex? Whatever. It felt so good, and we shared this pleasure every time we were alone. It got even better when at Helen's suggestion we spent weekends shacked up in our private unwedded bliss in Washington, D. C. Now that was really great.

In the beginning, I always used a condom. However, I dropped the encumbrance and doubled the pleasure after Helen told me that her doctor had told her that she couldn't get pregnant again. What the doctor may well have meant was that she *shouldn't* get pregnant again because of a history of miscarriages resulting from an incompatible RH factor with her late husband.

Then it happened. About mid-November, Helen told me that she had missed her period. My immediate reaction to his news was focused on marriage to Helen. The sex part of our relationship was great, but I had some doubts about our entering into a lifetime union. These doubts were reinforced by Bob and John, both of whom advised against marriage. They even said that if Helen brought the matter to court, they would be willing to testify that they had had sex with her, which would in those pre-DNA testing days cloud the paternity issue. Since both men were married, I'm not sure they would have carried through on this promise, but it did reinforce my doubt about the wisdom of marrying Helen. Sometime before Helen's dropped her bombshell, I had let John borrow my car to take Helen out on a date. This in itself suggested that I may not have been head over heels in love with her. After that date, Helen told me that John had tried to make out with her but that she had turned him down, knowing that he was a married man.

Finally, I became convinced that I was the father if Helen was indeed pregnant. My first thoughts focused on having the baby raised properly as a Christian. Although Helen was raised as a Methodist, I wasn't sure that she would be as concerned about church membership as I would want her to be with *my child*. I had a long talk with Helen after a Thanksgiving dinner that she and Jean had put on for Bob and me, and convinced her that there was no difference between our churches that she would object to. This knocked down a hurdle that might have stood in the way of a solid marriage.

Once I'd decided that the proper thing to do was to marry Helen, I wrote to my lady friend in Bay City to advise her of my decision. She wrote back to request that I return the picture she had given me, which I did.

Helen said she wanted us to get married in Maryland, not in Virginia or the District of Columbia, both of which were fine with me. It wasn't until many years later that I found out the reason for Helen's insistence on Maryland. That state did not require a blood test, which would have revealed the presence of syphilis that had been introduced into her body by her late husband.

After a wonderful weekend in DC, I returned to Ft. Eustis and Helen went to Baltimore to make arrangements for our wedding in a Lutheran church. She also obtained the marriage license and bought our wedding rings.

Meanwhile, Jean Syfert had returned from the Pacific and Bob reluctantly bowed out of the picture when Jean decided to stay with her husband.

It was on a Friday evening when Helen drove with the Syferts to the main gate where I was waiting to deliver her *good news.* "I had my period," she happily announced, "I'm not pregnant!" I was happy to hear this, I guess. What I failed to do or even consider doing was to scrap the nuptials, which were based on Helen's supposed pregnancy.

I felt certain that Helen loved me, but I couldn't say that I felt the same way about her at that time. My love for her grew over the course of several years. Now that the basic reason for getting married was removed, I should have announced that I didn't feel enough love for Helen to marry her at that point. The marriage would probably never have happened. There would probably been some hurt feelings at the moment, but this course of action would have saved Helen, both of our families and other innocents a lot of heartache many years later.

I suppose that my inability to change plans, to go with the flow, to leave decision making up to the inertial force generated by The Plan, contributed to my being swept along with the current that led to the altar. As in many other instances, I simply could not seem to alter a plan of action in light of changed circumstances. Moreover, it is possible that the fact that I had put off having sex for so many years vested my affair with Helen with a decisive "first love" power that it didn't deserve.

Only later did it occur to me that Helen may have fabricated a notional pregnancy to trick me into making a commitment to marriage without revealing her plan to anyone, not even to her sister. If that were the case, the web of deceit she wove certainly had tragic consequences.

Lest I leave the impression that ours was an unromantic marriage let me recall an afternoon somewhere east of San Francisco when we were on our extended honeymoon. Quite out of the blue, Helen pointed to a high hill about a mile from the paved road. She thought that would be a nice place to make love. We drove up to the end of the road, got out and walked quickly to the top of a knoll where we spread a blanket and quickly took off our clothes. We could watch the cars traveling on the road far below and the possibility of their watching us provided an extra measure of excitement as we joined our bodies. I had a better view of the road below while Helen had a better view of the beautiful azure sky above us. Afterwards, we rested right there on the fresh green grass, joined by a blissful oneness enhanced by the open beauty of the place. And we were relieved that no one had chanced to visit the place while we were there. In Paradise.

4

Career and Marriage

The military, family and career—the main ingredients in my physical existence, got sort of chopped up and mixed together in an existential blender set on low speed.

I had written Mother to tell her of my impending marriage, but apparently this early warning failed to soften the blow. When I called Mother, she seemed surprised and shocked by the news. Worse, she indicated disappointment at being unable to attend her son's wedding. That hurt. Talking with my bride whom she had never meet, by telephone, was obviously a less cordial situation than we would have wished. After their brief conversation, Helen said that Mother had been very cool, and that she was not exactly looking forward to their forthcoming face to face meeting. This happened a few weeks later. I had completed my training course at Ft. Eustis on December 7, 1951, and we left the following day for San Francisco via Bay City, Michigan. (We drove my car, because I wanted to hold onto it so that I'd have transportation in case the marriage didn't work out. Helen graciously sold her car—a year later model than mine—to pay off her personal debts, which she didn't want to bring with her into the marriage. I loved her for that!)

After we left Helen's daughter, Brenda, with her grandmother, Eva Morris, we drove all day and arrived at Mother's doorstep in the dark of night. Mother had moved upstairs and was renting out the downstairs apartment. The greetings exchanged between Helen and Mother were proper but restrained. Meetings with the rest of the List family in Bay City, where Uncle Will threw a party with his children and their spouses, and in Frankenmuth, were both cordial and relaxed. Helen especially liked Aunt Gustie in Frankenmuth.

Our drive to California was beset with cold weather and some hazardous road conditions. On our first day we got a late start and only got as far as Battle Creek, where Mother used to work as a nurse at the Sanitarium, Dr. John Harvey Kellogg's high colonic health center, enema capital of the world. We stayed overnight at the Hart Hotel across the street from the Seventh Day Adventist temple, which was somehow connected to the San, as Kellogg's spa was called by the locals. Our departure was delayed by a battery frozen dead in the parking lot, which required a jump start.

Eventually, we got to Tumcumcari, New Mexico. We heard on the radio that there had been a huge snow storm in the Central Rockies that had actually stalled a train in the area of the Donner Pass. We felt fortunate to be well to the south of that area, but an unexpected cold snap had covered dthe roads with snow and I had to geet a set of chains dto put on the rear tires. A few miles down the road, however, the snow was melted by sunlight, and we noisily bumped along until the noise got too much for us and I had to pull over and remove the chains. The next generation of motorists, who wee able to get tires with studs or, later, all-weather treads would never know the physical strain and mental stress of attaching and removing tire chains.

A few hours down the road, a sheet of ice suddenly coated the road on a steep incline and I wished that I had the chains back on again. There was a hill along the left side of the highway and a steep drop off on the right side with nothing but ice in between. The shoulder was indistinguishable from the nevertheless, I was determined to drive on, passing cars that had perhaps wisely pulled off to the side of the road. We reached the crest of the hill, I shifted into low gear, said a little prayer and we started down the other side. Maintaining a constant speed, I managed to avoid skidding and thought to myself that perhaps it was good that the tires were free of chains that might have acted like ice skates and put us over the edge. At the bottom, Helen and I breathed a deep sigh of relief and said of short prayer of thanksgiving. Perhaps our good fortune on the mountain was an omen of good things to come in the next few days as we moved into San Francisco and a brand new year: 1952.

We celebrated New Year's Eve in the ballroom of the Mark Hopkins Hotel followed by an ad hoc celebration in the room of some people we had met in the ballroom. The champagne flowed and all was well with the world.

Our good fortune continued as we quickly found a rental apartment on the south side of town that suited our needs to a tee. The owners were a Navy couple. He had been called to active duty, just as I had and, like me, planned to leave the military in about nine months. Perfect timing.

Meanwhile, in the Personnel Office at Fort Mason I checked in with the pretty young ladies I had never had a chance to ask for a date. All of my records had to be updated to include my changed marital status. I got the good news that I would henceforth receive a housing allowance.

Another perk of military life—free dental care—turned out to be an unpleas-ant experience for me when I went with Helen to have several of her teeth extracted. I waited in an outer room while the procedure was done, and later a nurse asked me to come in and help Helen get up and walk around to overcome the effect of the sodium pentathol, which had been used as an anesthetic. We had walked only a few steps when I started to feel faint as I thought of how painful the extractions must have been for my wife. The nurse recognized my symptoms and led me to a room where I could lie down and be brought back to the real world with some smelling salts. Compassion—shared suffering—must have caused my near blackout.

On Saturday nights, we frequently went to the Officers Club at the Naval Base on Treasure Island, which had been the site of the 1939-40 San Francisco Worlds Fair. Good and reasonably priced meals were served followed by dancing. The Army officers club at Fort Mason was lower key until it got a liquor license that kicked off a massive party one Saturday night. The band was swinging, the slot machines, which subsidized the price of food and drink, were clanging, and bar tenders mixed drinks with a minimum of mix, which they claimed was more expensive than the tax-free booze. WE felt no pain that night, and Helen later told me that my old buddy, John, had tried to persuade her to leave me that night.

Mother came out for a visit in the early spring. We dined at the Treasure Island Officers Club and visited relatives, including Erwin Greifenddorf and his live-in boyfriend. This odd couple took us along to parties that were friendly by somewhat different than what I was used to being a part of. Very interesting.

We had intended to attend an Easter sunrise service at Fleischhaker Park, but when the alarm clock sounded I got up and shut it off, since I didn't want to dis-turb the girls, who were sleeping soundly. When we finally woke up and the sun was high in the sky, we made our way to a post-sunrise service at Saint Pauls.

We did attend concerts at Fleischhaker Park, where one brought a box lunch and sat on the lawn as close as possible to the stage shell. On the recommenda-tion of Erwin and his friend, we went to Richard Strauss' light opera, *Der Rosen-kavalier*. In this lively farce, women pretend to be men and vice versa to the great amusement of the audience and very possibly the actors and some members of the audience as well. Our cultural enjoyment was also enriched by a production of Madame Butterfly at the beautiful San Francisco Opera House.

We also got to attend a concert by Judy Garland, at the top of her long career. Helen was a great fan of Judy's and was thrilled to shake her hand, when Judy graciously remained on stage after her performance to greet her many fans. I can't imagine a contemporary rock groups doing this for their idolaters.

Another sharp turn occurred in the straight line path I had planned for my life, when I opted for the second time in my life to leave the Army behind me. Originally, I had signed up for 21-24 months of active duty, but new rules were issued. We could be discharged after serving 17 months or re-enlist for an extended period of service, which would increase one's chance of being sent overseas. Helen and I discussed what I should do. I was eager to return to Ernst & Ernst to complete my pursuit of a CPA certificate, which would open the door to making it big in the corporate world out there. Helen fully supported this plan. I think she was tired as I was of constantly moving around, which was a way of life in the armed forces. Little did we realize that we would be moving as much or more in the civilian sector.

Our first trip after my discharge in mid-April 1952 put us on Route sixty-six headed east. Mother came along with us, which led to some unpleasantness between my two ladies. I tried but failed to keep them on an even, friendly keel. Our first stop was in Las Vegas, where we enjoyed a performance by ex-pat Josephine Baker. At Helen's suggestion I was in uniform, and we were promptly moved to the head of a long line to be ushered to a stage-side table. I felt some mixed emotions about having to put my uniform—a pass to many deserved privileges—into moth balls. In New Mexico, we encountered a rather unpleasant family crossroad. Helen and I decided that since we were so near to them, we might as well pay a visit to Helen's sister, Jean, and her husband, who lived in San Angelo, Texas. This improvised change in our itinerary upset Mother, who decided to split and fly back to Bay City alone. We continued our journey without the benefit of Mother's company.

In "dear old Ann Arbor town," as it's called in the college song "I wanna go back to Meechigan," I was showing Helen around when I was hailed by an Auditing Professor of mine. This prof, who had recommended me for my internship with Ernst and Ernst, told me that Ford motor Co. was determined to overtake Chevrolet in car sales and was expanding their accounting department. He advised me to check out this opportunity for a job that would offer higher pay than I could expect at E & E. I had already made up my mind, however, and no wise old professor, however well-meaning, was going to change it. Moreover, Helen supported my career plan. So after a side trip to Newport News, where we picked up Helen's daughter Brenda to live with us, we headed back to Michigan. And I was back with dear old E & E.

One of my first audit assignments was at the Packard Motor Car Co. in Detroit. On this nearly three-year assignment, I found that my health was not the best and that the financial health of a company did not always reflect the quality of its product.

Shortly after taking up residence in Highland Park I came down with a strep throat infection that kept me housebound for a week. Helen was able to get a doctor to come to our second floor apartment to examine me and prescribe medicine. This fine Jewish man, a dedicated healer became our family doctor.

My career prospects appeared to rise, not least because of diligent study on my own time. I succeeded in passing the second part of the CPA exam after I'd been employed by E & E for two years. Helen provided encouragement and a good study environment for me. After flunking and having to retake the audit part of the exam, I passed the final exam in November 1954. I received the good news by telegram. Those who failed were notified by mail.

My marriage prospects, unfortunately, were less promising for several reasons. First there was the continuous stress of Helen's miscarriages. It's not that she didn't want to carry her pregnancies to term. Once, when a doctor advised her that she had "aborted," Helen exclaimed that she had done nothing to cause the loss of the fetus. The doctor explained that the term "aborted" merely meant the early loss of the fetus by whatever cause. During her pregnancies, I had to take Helen to the doctor rather often, usually in the evening or on Saturday. At the doctor's, Helen took a series of shots, which I assumed were related to the Rh factor problem that we knew about. Years later, when we were in Rochester, NY, Helen admitted to me that the shots were related to the syphilis that she had contracted in Korea from her husband.

Life in Highland Park and later in the suburb of Inkster was a topo map of hills and valleys. In Inkster, thought by those who were ticketed while driving through it on the main highway (US 12) as the worst speed trap in Michigan, we bought a nice three bedroom free-standing house on a slab. This was the first house we purchased, and we were elated by the special pride that accompanies home ownership. The houses stood on long, narrow lots, and perhaps in line with the old adage that fences make good neighbors, four or five neighbors got together to construct fences on our lot lines. We all pitched in, shared our labor as well as rental tools. This old-fashioned barn-raising spirit created great neighborhood camaraderie.

Earlier in Highland Park, we had moved to strengthen our family's religious unity. Helen had taken instruction in the Lutheran teachings at a small mission church in San Francisco and had been confirmed there. When we joined the congregation in Highland Park I wrote to the San Francisco pastor to request a letter of transfer to our new religious home. He never responded, but our elderly pastor accepted my wife into membership anyway. My membership had been transferred from Zion in Bay City. Helen and I both sang in the choir. I taught Sunday school and Brenda attended a Lutheran elementary school on the church grounds. In Inkster, we joined a relatively new Lutheran church where Helen had demonstrated her faith in a special way. A lady from a large Negro housing development on the other side of the highway came to attend our church and was ignored by most of the congregation. Helen went out of her way to talk with this woman and make her feel welcome. One day the pastor came to our home to thank Helen for her kindness. Helen, who grew up in North Carolina, explained that she felt comfortable talking with the lady because she had been happy as a child when she was cared for by a black lady when her mother was at work.

Unfortunately, the good things that blessed our family were overshadowed by some negatives in our marriage. After we had been in Highland Park for several months, Helen told Brenda and me that she didn't think our marriage would work out. Both Brenda and I were saddened to hear this and were both brought to the brink of tears. I had come to love Helen and to feel comfortable in our life together. The prospect of divorce filled me with a sense of shame, since mine would be the first ever in the List family. The same would apply to Helen.

In retrospect I can find several reasons why Helen my have felt that our marriage didn't live up to her expectations, not least the physical and psychological stress caused by her frequent miscarriages. There must also have been stress produced by her knowing that she had syphilis and had to keep this secret from me.

I'm sure that our lifestyle was more quiet and sedate than what she had experienced with her late husband. Gone were the NCO clubs (her husband had been a sergeant) with their cheap food and drink, dancing and slot machines. No longer could she go to the movies, which she loved, for 15 cents. In short, we had to live on a tighter budget in civilian life than Helen had grown accustomed to as an Army wife. I also suspect that alcohol played a large role in our downgraded life style.

In the Army it was not only socially acceptable but almost standard Operating Procedure to have a few belts before dinner at the Officers Club, often followed by after dinner drinks and a highball or two "for the road." I didn't think too much of this in the Army. I enjoyed a friendly drink as much as anyone. But after our move into civilian life, I was worried by the way Helen needed more than just a few drinks. When she went shopping, a bottle of whiskey often came home in her shopping bag. After a while it became obvious that Helen was hooked on a deadly poison. This was apparent even to Brenda, who told me that her mother was sneaking drinks all day long while I was at work.

I asked Helen to stop or at least cut down on her drinking and she invariably promised to do so, but invariably went back to the bottle. Sometimes I secretly tried to water down the booze. Nothing worked. There was always something to celebrate, which called for just a social drink…or two. Sometimes it got ugly.

On a New Year's Eve, we were invited to a neighbor's home for a party. Helen had talked me into bringing home a bottle for the holiday, and by the time we left for the party at nine o'clock she was well on her way down the slippery slope. Walking to the neighbors, I had to support Helen. When we got there, Helen planted herself on a sofa between the host and another neighbor. Our host gave her a kiss that I considered improper, and to his surprise, I slugged him. Whereupon, the men went to the kitchen and the ladies took me to a bedroom. I was told that I had best go home, which I did. Helen came home much later. I only wish I'd known about AA at the time.

I may well have been anxious about Helen and our marriage at that time, but I only recall one incident that suggested the possibility of a serious condition. It happened at a gas station in Port Huron, where I was working on an audit of Ironite Co. I was filling up my car when I suddenly experienced a mental blackout. Quite suddenly and without any warning, I wondered where I was and what I was doing there. I didn't think about my marriage; nor did I think about combat in WW II. My mind simply froze.

Some rather radical changes in my family and employment situations occurred in the mid-50's. First, Patricia Marie "Patty" List first saw the light of day on January 9, 1955. As a middle name, she was given one of my mother's middle names.

On October 21, 1956, John Frederick List II was born, named after my father. Helen had wanted to have my son named John Emil, but I objected. Although I dearly loved my uncle Emil, I was never comfortable with his name and never used it except as required for legal documentation.

At about this time, I was advised by E & E that my performance wasn't up to their expectations. This happened just a few months after I had passed my CPA exam, and took me by surprise. I was too startled and shy to ask in what area my performance was found lacking. Had I done so, I might have been able to correct a particular shortcoming, which could have helped me to succeed in later years. The blow was cushioned by my employer promising to help me get a position with another employer. I knew that normally they would get a job for a departed employee at a firm where one of their alumni was located.

I was too ashamed to tell Helen that I was being fired. Instead, I told her that I'd decided it was time for me to get a job in an industrial corporation where I could get higher pay. In fact, I might have decided to move on voluntarily, since I was still convinced that I should be able to move up to a higher position; e.g., controller or treasurer of a large corporation.

Soon an interview was set up for me at Sutherland Paper Co. in Kalamazoo, whose Controller, Bernard "Bernie" White, had worked at E & E. Sutherland was a family-owned business, and the founder was still semi-active when I started work there. The President and Chief Operating Officer came from England and was, coincidentally I'm sure, married to the founder's daughter.

When I got to Sutherland, which paid for my moving expenses, I was put in charge of auditing and taxes. The top financial officers, Controller and Financial VP, together with the auditors handled most of the work on federal taxes. I managed the reporting to various states where we conducted taxable business. Later I was transferred to head up a large part of the cost accounting department, which kept track of the production of paperboard cartons. This enabled me to get out into the plant more, which I enjoyed.

The first of the four houses we occupied in Kalamazoo was a large, old rental property on the south side of the city. Next came a duplex on the northeast side of town, in the other half of which lived a dentist, whose wife always insisted he be called "doctor." Helen informed the lady that her husband was not an M.D. and, therefore, should not be called "Doctor," which had a chilling effect on inter-duplex relations.

At about the same time that Frederick Michael was born, we moved back to the south side of *Kazoo,* as the natives called their city, where we rented a pleasant house on a corner lot. After that we bought a house further south on a street named "Lover's Lane," which was a real misnomer, as our love life was definitely on the wane. I don't know if this was caused by the stress of handling a growing family, our frequent housing moves, Helen's failing health and alcohol abuse or simply the erosion of romance caused by the passage of time I don't know. Whatever the cause, we were aware of the slippage and looked for ways to get our sex act back on track. I bought sexually stimulating "blue" movies at adult only shops and by mail order. No kinky stuff, just variations on straight sex, but these failed to accomplish their advertised purpose. But we kept trying. At our next location in Rochester, NY, we bought a Polaroid camera with which we took pictures of ourselves in sexually explicit positions and bought photos of other couples making love in multiple positions. We considered going one step further by finding another couple who wanted to swap partners. We received a mail response by one couple, but decided against going through with it, probably because we both felt we were too likely to become jealous.

Some years later Helen played the jealousy card by telling me that one of the tops execs at Xerox was having an affair with her, coming to our home to enjoy a matinee. I seriously doubted this, but must have had doubts, because on several occasions I drove by our house to see if there was a strange car parked in the driveway. I then confronted Helen and she had to admit there was no affair.

As Helen's condition worsened in later years, it became increasingly difficult for her to reach orgasm, and this in turn made intercourse less pleasant for me. At one point in Rochester, I might have been tempted to have an affair with a very tall, slender and attractive blond secretary. But I was held back by my moral opposition to extramarital sex and the effect it my have on the children. Finally, there was lack of time and, perhaps most importantly, insufficient funds to be able to carry on an affair with flare.

Although my health was generally good, I did suffer a hernia problem one spring, which I had repaired at the hospital only to have a second hernia develop from shoveling heavy, wet snow from the driveway. After some days in the hospital I returned home, and was under orders to avoid any abdominal strain. Since Helen didn't drive, I had to drive our stick-shift car to the store to buy food supplies. Shifting gears and toting bags of groceries went beyond limits the doctor had prescribed, but I recovered and had no more hernia problems. There were, however, other problems.

Since she didn't drive, Helen didn't come to visit me in the hospital. After I got home, Brenda told me that her mother had been hitting the whiskey bottle in my absence. I don't remember whether she had the stuff delivered to the house or if she called the store to order the wet goods (as W.C. Fields called his liquor supply) for Brenda to pick up and bring home.

I continued to be an active church member in Kalamazoo, serving as a member of the Council and Treasurer at Zion Lutheran Church. Pastor Grother recalls that he and I "became good friends, but not the kind that shared great intimacy in what we thought and where we wanted to go professionally." Unfortunately, Helen seemed to lose interest in church. In a letter to me in prison, Pastor Grother remembers that he made a great effort "to involve Helen in happy worship of God and in friendship with God with ladies in the church…seeking especially to get her active in the Ruth Guild that met evenings. My ladies complained that she just didn't seem to desire close friendship, and found reasons not to be a part of the group."

Although she was inactive in the church, Helen supported, albeit passively, my efforts to establish a religious foundation for the upbringing of our children. This was never an area of real conflict. Our problems stemmed from our personalities having been shaped in different environments. For example, when I was growing up, my parents never spoke harshly to each other in my presence. While I found the venting of disputes to be unsettling, Helen seemed to enjoy verbal confrontations, which she claimed helped to clear the air.

One of Helen's pet themes was that I was too much under the thumb of my mother. Of course, I didn't see it that way. Once at the dinner table, I guess I reached the point where I could take no more. I lifted my end of the table, which probably caused some dishes to slide off onto the floor and stalked out of the house. I walked around the neighborhood for some time and then returned to the house briefly before leaving for a Council meeting at church. The children were probably upset by my outburst, and I'm sure I later apologized. But Helen didn't harp on the subject of my early upbringing after that.

During our residence on Lover's Lane, Helen's 16-year-old daughter, Brenda, got pregnant. We located a Florence Crittenden facility in Jackson, a two-hour drive from Kalamazoo, where the baby was born and given up for adoption. I visited Brenda several times to boost her morale. Helen had several reasons for not coming with me. It hurt her too much to see Brenda suffer and we didn't want to take our small children to see her.

Brenda eventually married the father of their baby, but their marriage was in almost constant trouble, and they frequently lived apart from each other.

Our Patty, who was three or four years old at the time, commented that Brenda had certainly messed up her life. I wonder if Patty would have acted the same way at that age. Sadly, she died before she reached Brenda's age. Patty was 16 years and 10 months old at the time of her death.

Meanwhile, back at Sutherland we had merged with Parchment paper Co. located a few miles northeast of Kalamazoo. The top management of the merged company worked at Parchment, which meant that the elimination of duplicate jobs would favor those who held positions with the major partner and headroom for promotions would shrink. The writing on the wall was all too clear. Time for John List to look for greener pastures, which I did covertly, mailing out resumes and making up stories to cover my absences when I went to interview for jobs with Carrier Corp., Texas Instruments, IBM, and Haloid Corp. in Rochester, NY.

IBM soon offered me a position as a cost accountant, but this offer was soon topped by a bid for my services from Haloid with a salary of $12,000 per year, three thousand more than I was making at Sutherland, and a loftier job title. It didn't take long to opt for accepting a position as Asst. Mgr. of General Accounting, with one of the hottest corporations in the country. Hadloid, which in a short space of time became Hadloid-Xerox and, finally Xerox, had operating revenues of $37 million in 1960 and $528 million in 1966. In the decade of the sixties, the company's payroll would jump from 2,000 to 55,000 employees. I was excited to be a part of this dynamic corporation, and so was Helen, who couldn't wait to move into the big time corporate world. When she joined me for my second interview on the invitation of the controller, Clint Hutto, we were given a rather seedy room in one of the city's better hotels. Helen was shocked. At her prodding, I called the desk and got an upgrade. Later that weekend, when we had gotten to know Clint a little better, Helen told him that she thought the company should get good rooms to make a positive impression on their future employees. Clint accepted the constructive criticism graciously. Of course it might have helped that he grew up in South Carolina, a stone's throw from Helen's home town of Greensboro, North Carolina.

Xerox is Greek for "dry," which refers to the copier process in which powder is fused to the company's special Xeroxagraphic copy paper. All Xerox copier machines were leased to the users at that time. The leasee had to send in a monthly report of the reading on a counter that recorded how many copies had been made by each machine. This created a huge volume of data which had to be entered into the computer system, which required new programs to handle newer, faster, more efficient equipment. Problems had to be solved on the run, which created new problems and customer complaints. The upshot of all this was that the Billing Section came under the greatest pressure for improvement. (Eventually, this section had to use a separate group of more experienced employees to deal with chronic problems.) Shortly after I started work at Xerox, I was promoted to be Manager of Accounting, which included the Billing Section as well as the General Accounting and Cost Accounting sections. The pressure to grow and perform at the speed of light required long hours on the job. Ten to twelve hour days were not unusual. Saturday was treated as a normal weekday and 60- to 70-hour work weeks were common.

In this pressure cooker situation, Helen's mysterious physical ailments that first caused her to be hospitalized in Kalamazoo reappeared. Doctors were unable to diagnose the debilitating illness, and she was eventually referred to a psychiatrist. Helen made appointments for Saturday mornings so that I could drive her to the doctor, but she never reported to me of what transpired in his office. After a few visits, she decided to discontinue her consultations with the psychiatrist.

Helen had been active in the Altar Guilds of several churches, but this commitment declined to zero at Zion, where the children and I did both the Holy Communion preparation and clean-up work.

Helen's declining energy level was also evident at home, where she spent more and more time in bed. I did all of the grocery shopping and often I had to prepare super when I returned from work, or in my absence, Patty made the evening meal. When I had to return to the office, as often happened, the children had to wash the dishes. Sometimes, Patty and I had to do the family laundry work.

Amazingly, Helen perked up and seemed her normal self on certain occasions, such as when we went shopping for a new car. Helen felt that in my position at Xerox, I should have a higher class car, so we went car shopping and bought a Dodge 880 with a push-button transmission that I really liked.

Helen also got up for our trips to Europe and Mexico, when I attended company meetings. Rank-Xerox, the global corporation, graciously paid for officers' wives to come along on these trips for R & R. Helen and I decided to use our pre-conference vacation week to do some sightseeing in our ancestral homelands of Ireland and Germany. The Xerox travel office handled the tickets and reservations and the medical department handled the required immunization shots.

We first toured western Ireland where we stumbled into an office building in Galway that housed the local constabulary. When he learned that Helen's family came from the area, one of the officers gave us a guided tour that included a segregated cemetery that kept Protestants on one side and Catholics on the other side. Helen corresponded with this congenial Irish guide for years to come.

En route to Germany we stopped in Dublin long enough for Helen to buky some Waterford crystal, some Irish plaid fabric for dresses and two plaques embossed with the Morris family coat of arms.

Lufthansa, the national airline of what was then the Federated Republic of [West] Germany, took us to Frankfurt am Main. We arrived late and had to order food from room service. Expensive? Sure, but what did we care. Xerox picked up the hotel bill. The next morning we drove off in our Volkswagen rental car and I must have thought we were still in the UK, for I quickly found myself driving into oncoming traffic on a congested one-way street. A clanging street car and cars with angry fist-waving drivers let me know that I should turn my outweighed Volkswagen around—or die. This led me onto the no-speed-limit Autobahn to compete with my aggressive German cousins. The first time I tried to pass a car, bright headlights flashed in my rearview mirror to signal the approach of a Mercedes doing about 160 Km/hr, who wanted me to get back in my right-hand lane—or die!

In Bavaria, we visited with several of my distant cousins in an area that I had passed through as an enemy soldier 20 years before. The irony continued when I learned that our host at a family reunion in the little town of Rosstal had flown with Goering's Luftwaffe during the war. When I told him that Helen came from the south and I from the North, he made the analogy of his roots being in Bavaria while his wife came from Prussia in the northeast corner of Germany. Her grandmother commented "We used to fight each other, now we marry each other instead." Just like Helen and I.

Before leaving Germany, we visited the Black Forest, where we purchased a coo-coo clock and had it shipped back home, and the historic city of Worms, best known as the site of Martin Luther's defense of his "heretical" beliefs. We were met at London's Heathrow airport by our Rank-Xerox hosts and driven in a Bentley to our hotel. It was either Claridges or The Dorchester. (When you're traveling first class you don't bother remembering such minutiae.)

Helen was invited to join other wives on tours, including the Rank movie set and Herrod's department store. She declined these invitations on the grounds of illness, but she refused to see a doctor. (When years later I met with Helen's sister, Jean Syfert, I asked her why she thought Helen had declined to join the other wives. She commented that Helen would never be interested in attending all-female event of that sort.)

One evening our Rank Group hosts took a group of us to tour Parliament followed by a sumptuous multi-course dinner with different wines served with each course. After all of our meetings were over, we headed back home. On our flight from New York to Rochester our Electra developed an engine problem and we diverted to Buffalo. We took a bus to Rochester where we arrived in the wee hours of the morning, tired but happy with what had been a wonderful trip and happier still to be together with the children and Mother, who had cared for them in our absence.

Back at the office I was embarrassed to find that several of my colleagues had brought back gifts for their secretaries. I had never thought of doing that.

At about that time I was given an assignment that I hated. Clint had ordered me to fire and old time Xerox employee in accounting who wasn't working up to speed in our fast-moving concern. He was a nice, friendly person, and I tried to explain to him that I personally liked him but that he imply wasn't performing up to our requirements. He was nonplussed and I felt terrible. Fortunately, this old timer knew the executives who were there when the company was small and he probably got these good old boys to get him job in the Finance Division. I wondered later if Clint gave me the job of firing this man to test my skill as an executive.

Fortunately, I didn't have to fire any more employees but became quite heavily involved in the company's hiring of new personnel, which required travel to interview prospective recruits in Chicago and elsewhere. I also attended career-enhancing seminars at company expense, including a course in "Brainstorming" at the University of Buffalo.

I was, in short, riding the crest of a wave in my profession and loving it, especially the managerial perks involving paid vacations to exotic places. After Europe, Helen and I flew to Mexico City a few days before company meetings there. We were met at the airport by the chief of Rank-Xerox operations in Mexico, Mr. Smith, whose Latino features contradicted his Anglo name. We stayed at the plush Maria Isabella on Paseo de la Forma, or rather we used our suite there as a base for sightseeing. I again rented a VW "Bug," which took us through a series of peasant villages with central squares all the way to the pyramids north of the capital. There small boys sold us "pre-Columbian" statuettes that were probably no more than two days old. Then on a to a charming cantina where we made the mistake of ordering *leche* (milk). The next morning we awoke to *Montezuma's Revenge*, which prevented me from making my first meeting. Helen got the hotel doctor to prescribe a medication that cured her.

One evening, Stu Ames of the Budget Department, Helen and I dined at the Smith home, where excellent food was served by several girls, followed by a visit to the magnificent National Opera House. Finally, we visited a night club where a top-flight dance team from Spain performed a breath-taking dance. It was downright exciting. Like my career, which had reached a level I had never dreamed of achieving. On the sunny side of forty, I was clarly a success. I was totally unaware of the storm clouds building on my professional horizon.

The managers at Xerox frequently lunched together, which provided an opportunity for us to get to know each other, to develop some sort of *team chemistry*, as they say in the sports world. Sometimes our chief, Clint Hutto, would join the group and sometimes he would take an individual manager to lunch to discuss a particular issue. When it came my turn Clint and I had a general discussion over lunch accompanied by several drinks. As we approached our office building, Clint turned to me and said in a matter of fact manner, "You understand that you have to get rid of Helen." I was stunned and probably mumbled some sort of innocuous reply like "Yes." I should have made and appointment to see him and find out what he was referring to with his remark. I couldn't recall ever having discussed my marital life with the man, and I couldn't think of any reason for him to come out of the blue with such a statement.

At about this time, there was another conference with Rank-Xerox people. I wasn't involved in any of the working sessions, and as far as I knew neither were any of the other managers in the Control Division. We did attend a joint dinner. Helen and I were assigned to one of the outer rooms in the banquet hall. Helen intuited that I was being pushed aside, out of the managerial mainstream. But I thought that our seating was only designed to spread the managers around. Unfortunately, she was right.

Shortly afterwards, Clint called me in to tell me that he felt I couldn't keep pace with the growth of the company and that my services wee no longer required.

Before I was hired at Xerox, I had been interviewed by a psychiatrist who worked as a consultant with Battelle, a company that had close corporate ties to Xerox. The same psychiatrist had interviewed me during my employment with Xerox and saw me again when I was fired. After this final interview, he told me that I wasn't very well suited to work in the environment of a rapidly growing company, and recommended that I join a less volatile firm. (In the nearly four years I spent with Xerox, our sales grew from $60 million to $250 million.)

The door didn't hit my backsides as I left Xerox. In fact, I was assisted in finding a new position. In addition to psychiatric counseling, Xerox softened my exit landing by providing me full pay and a private room from which to conduct my job search. Clint even tried to get me a job in the Finance Division, but they didn't want me, possibly because of ill feeling harbored by the Old Guard employee I had fired who ended up in Finance. (*What goes around, comes around,* as they say and nowhere is this adage more true than in the dog-eat-dog corporate world.)

Despite management's help, it took several months for me to find work. Most likely, potential employers would wonder why anyone would leave a company like Xerox if they were competent. I tried to explain that I wanted an opportunity to advance to the position of Controller, and that the experience I had gained at Xerox would be beneficial to a future employer.

I suppose Clint was under some pressure to get me off the premises and the payroll. He occasionally dropped by to ask me how it was going in my search for a new position. In any case I was treated better than personnel fired in later years, when, according to the testimony of Pastor Saresky at my trial, discharged employees were informed of being fired, then escorted to their office to remove personal property from their desks and shown the door.

Several years after I moved to Westfield, New Jersey, Clint called to see how I was doing. He had also left Xerox, which may or may not have been voluntary, and was working with a company in Chicago, though he still lived outside Rochester. I probably should have asked him if he had a job for me, but I suppose I was satisfied with what I had at the time. After my incarceration I learned that Clint had died of cancer.

I was in Chicago to interview prospective employees for Xerox, when the news reported that President Kennedy had been shot. All appointments for the afternoon were cancelled. Although I didn't much like him as President, I did shed some tears during his funeral, especially when the riderless horse came by. I don't really know if the tears were for JFK or sorrow for all the men who were killed in World War II and Korea.

5

Post Xerox—A Professional Slalom

As a result of the resumes I sent out from the workspace provided by Xerox, I had a promising interview, followed by an offer of a position with the First National Bank of Jersey City, New Jersey. The salary of $25,000 per annum was about what I had been earning at Xerox, and I was elevated to the position of Vice President and Comptroller. The bank was located on a large square on the banks of the Hudson River, right across from the exciting skyline of the financial heart of America.

It was a rather large gamble going to work for a bank, but I was optimistic that I cold handle the challenge. After all, I rationalized, I'd taken a course in "Money and Banking" in college. Once I started work, however, I felt like a fish out of water. Contrary to the job title, the position was essentially a public relations job. The bank needed someone to develop new customers in the suburbs surrounding the old industrial cities in the northern part of the state. They had the wrong man and very soon both the bank and I knew it. After just a year on the job, I was given my walking papers.

In the beginning, as with my earlier positions, it looked great. I was given a cordial welcome and when the family joined me we were visited by the bank's VP for Personnel. He had recently joined the bank and he told us how happy he and his family were to be there. We were looking for a house in an area with a Lutheran church and day school and settled on the pleasant suburb of Westfield. With the help of a local realtor, we soon found a large Victorian house in a nice quiet neighborhood and were almost instantly hooked. It was a turn of the century mansion built by John Sammuel Augustus Wittke, a rich industrialist, located on a knoll on the highest point between the Wachung Mountains and the Port of Elizabeth. The wife and mother of the family who had live in the place with the romantic name of Breeze Knoll for decades had recently died.

Inside the house was a large open area, a sort of atrium. There was a grand staircase from the ground floor to the second floor and a smaller continuation to the third floor. The second floor of the mansion had five bedrooms. There was a two-section bathroom with a tub in one room and a toilet and vanity in an adjoining room. Our master bedroom had its own bath. The third floor consisted of four bedrooms, which I later converted into an apartment for Mother.

A stairway off the second sitting room on the main floor led down to a paneled Billiard Room. At the end of the 30'x 15' room there was a raised platform where the children sometimes staged impromptu plays. Later, when Pat was active in a school theatre group, the room was used for rehearsals. Above this room was the ball room, where there were beautiful stained glass windows like those seen in churches. Another attractive feature were fireplaces in the sitting rooms, the billiard and ballrooms, the dining room and each of the bedrooms.

The house stood on an acre and a quarter lot, and there ws a freestanding garage on the property. The front yard had stately pine trees, much like the ones I had always admired at Uncle Emil's place, bordering the drive leading ukp to the house. A magnolia tree just outside the master bedroom added a special touch, which Helen loved. Altogether it was an impressive piece of real estate, which we fell in love with.

O course the property had seen better days and was in need of repairs, which served to bring the price down close to our price range. Listed on the tax rolls at $100,000 the asking price had come down to $50,000! It was certainly a good deal.

However, what with moving expenses and buying top of the line clothes for the kids, we were a bit short of cash for the down payment on the mortgage. I had no qualms about asking Mother for a loan, and she readily agreed to help. I did not, however, suggest that Mother come to live with us. That was entirely Helen's idea. She noted that Mother had long expressed an interest in living closer to us, and we could easily convert the third floor into pleasant living quarters for her. I expressed reservations in light of past friction between my ladies, but Heln assured me that the arrangement would work, and it did for a while.

It wasn't long, however, before frictional issues arose. Helen reverted to spending more time in bed with her ailments, and Mother tried to help by doing the laundry and cooking some of the evening meals. At times she had one of the children up to her apartment to eat with her, which they seemed to enjoy, to the annoyance of Helen.

I pitched in by sharpening my culinary skills, including the preparation of chops and hamburgers on a cast iron grill. This would prove invaluable later in my new life.

In addition to her chronic lethargy, Helen sometimes had trouble breathing. There were times, especially at night, when Helen felt unable to breathe and would open the window and stick her head outside even in the winter. I had to close the bedroom door to prevent freezing the entire house. Finally, our doctor, a German immigrant referred Helen to a top neurologist at Columbia-Presbyterian in NYC. While she was there for tests, I took the subway to visit her on weekdays and drove in to visit on weekends. When she was released, Helen said that some atrophy had been found in part of heer brain caused by her attested syphilis. There was nothing, she said, to remedy this condition. I later thought that I should have insisted on tdaling with the specialist at Presbyterian. After leaving the hospital, Helen seemed quite well, and we lunched at the famous German restaurant Luchow's (which I had mistakenly thought was Lu Chou's, a Chinese restaurant). When we got home, Helen's health continued to improve. But it was not to last for long. She lost her appetite and became quite weak. At times she would fall down trying to get from her bed to the bathroom or window. It was easy for me to lift her back into bed because she had lost so much weight.

When the Syferts visited us on their way to Germany, Jean was shocked to find her sister in such bad health. It was probably at this time that I told Jean, as she later reported, that Helen had kept me from doing better in my jobs. Normally I kept that observation, however accurate it was, to myself. In any case, there was no doubt that my professional career was in a tailspin with n emergency landing field in sight.

After my "release" from the bank, I embarked on an intensive job search. It was easy for me to contact executive personnel search firms in New York, and in quiet desperation I borrowed money from Mother to pay a fee to one of these so-called "headhunter" agencies who guaranteed getting me a job. Before signing on with these people, I had interviews with the American Photography Company (APC), a holding company that owned several photo studios located in different department stores. By using a variety of trade names, APC could have studios in competing retail outlets.

I was in charge of all accounting, which was something like being asked to sort out a large can of worms. Since each studio was incorporated independently, each kept separate accounting statements, and all of this was down manually. We may have used NDR accounting machines, but it was a clumsy operation for such a high volume of records. After about a year of this, I asked for and was granted permission to convert the records to a computer. I thought that my experience at Xerox provided me with the expertise necessary to manage this transition, and I hired a man to head the rather massive records' transfer.

Apparently I failed to involve myself closely enough in supervising the conversion from manual to computer processing. I was suddenly confronted with errors and breakdowns of information needed to ensure control of the cash flow. Money from the studios had to be transferred periodically to APC accounts. The new system broke down and I was left with a mess on my hands. At the same time, the company moved from downtown Manhattan to Long Island where the owners and some managers lived. This posed a cumbersome commuting problem for me which combined with the accounting conversion problems to end my association with APC. My professional career had reached a dead end, but I was too proud—or ashamed—to admit it to my family or even to myself.

This deception had begun when I was released from the bank and didn't tell Helen or anyone else about it. She once called the bank to talk to me and was told that I was no longer there. This hurt, because it was the first time I had been dishonest with Helen. I tried to cover my firings by pretending to go to work every morning, wearing a suit and a tie and driving off in the only car we had left after I sold our second car. Sometimes I went to New York City to contact employment agencies and killed time at the city library between appointments. Some days I just stayed in the car at the railroad station.

During the layoffs at the bank and APC I had been too proud to apply for unemployment compensation, which would have cushioned my loss of income. Instead I had to take out a second mortgage on the house. Some of these funds were used to pay for remodeling of the third floor to provide Mother with her living space, but most of the money was needed to pay for the goods and services to maintain the image of prosperity that both Helen and I craved. It was an example of *conspicuous consumption* in the extreme. To cite one example: I replaced a small lamp in the foyer wit a large and expensive chandelier worthy of Versailles. My sister-in-law, Jean Syfert later told me that I tried too hard to please Helen by buying whatever caught he eye. No Doubt.

The final turn in my race to the bottom of the slalom slope of my career was life selling insurance. It started out well enough with the sale of a large policy to an oil executive who was an active church member and a Westfield neighbor. According to the sales formula, I was to get five leads from the satisfied customer and in this way the well of prospects would never run dry. But it did as I failed to convert any of my leads into sales. My General Agent, Burt Goldstein, gave me a loan of $500, which was like putting a band aid on a massive hemorhage.

On several occasions I borrowed funds from Mother in the form of checks drawn on her personal checking account to meet the most pressing of my financial needs. (Contrary to claims made by an unauthorized biographer, Mother kept control of her funds at all times.) At about the time that Mother said she could not afford to lend me any more money, I received a note from the savings and loan company that if my mortgage payments were not brought up to date they would have to foreclose on our home.

Financial problems were accompanied by problems of raising teenage children more or less by myself. A couple of painful real life incidents may illustrate the point.

One day I discovered Pat and some of her friends playing with a Ouija board. I asked them not to get involved in this sort of activity, which I had read could release destructive forces.

More disturbing was a phone call I received in the early morning hours on a Sunday. It came from the police station, where Pat and the Hansens' daughter were being held. I was told that the girls had been found wandering around the streets in the wee hours and had been picked up for their own protection. I was so angry with Pat that I couldn't say a word on our ride home. When we got home we went to the master bedroom where Helen and I both talked to Pat about her unacceptable behavior.

Apparently the girls had thought walking around in the dark was a "lark."

After church, Mr. Hansen berated me because he felt that it was Pat's fault that the girls were out on the town alone. I, of course, stood up for Pat and said that it was at least as much his daughter's fault.

On another occasion, I found a small snake on the sideboard of the kitchen stove. I didn't ask which of the children had put it there. I just picked it up with a BBQ fork and put it in the garbage can outside the kitchen door. I'm not certain what, if anything, the snake was meant to signify. But I can't believe that all three children *just happened to be in the kitchen* when I discovered the reptile. Normally, they would either have been in bed or upstairs getting washed. I have a hunch that Pat was at the bottom of the plot and had alerted the boys to come watch for possible fireworks.

In any case, the stage was set for the tragedy that was to follow.

John List seated beside his mother outside their home in Bay City, MI
(1947)

John List in uniform with Combat Infantry badge after his return from
World War II

(From left), Helen Taylor, Jean Syfert, and John List on October 13, 1951, the night they met outside a bowling alley in Fort Eustice, Va. Helen and John were married less than 2 months later.

The beaming new father, John List, with Patty, January, 1955.

Proud new grandmother, Alma List, shows off toddler Patty.

Helen List and her children, shortly after they moved to Westfield, New Jersey, in 1965.

John List in N.J. State prison (2001)

JOHN E LIST   Inmate Housing Location: New Jersey State Prison-Main
Male DOB: 09/17/1925   SBI #: 000303030A   Booking #: 225472

03/30/2001 - Internal Correspondence: Psychiatric assessment for inclusion in PTSD group
Provider: Arthur D. Boxer, MD
Location of Care: New Jersey State Prison
This document contains confidential information

Chart Note

Narrative: S: "I still have amnesia for periods of time when I was an infantry
man in Europe in WW II. I was a mortor gunner and just don't
remember. It really upsets me, but I can discuss this with
John Scally and I don't feel as upset."
O: Alert and verbal. No delusional thinking.
A: This man obviously feels better give a forum to discuss his
distress. He did not volunteer anything about the sentence he
is serving and was not pressed although I believe it weighs on
him and the apprehension years later.
P: Continue in John Scally's group. No psychotropics indicated.

PTSD Diagnosis signed by MD. March 1, 2004

JOHN E LIST   Inmate Housing Location: New Jersey State Prison-Main
Male DOB: 09/17/1925   SBI #: 000303030A   Booking #: 225472

05/17/2001 - Internal Other: MH Treatment Plan
Provider: David B. Starkey, PhD
Location of Care: New Jersey State Prison-Main
This document contains confidential information

Current Problems:
Hx of HEARING LOSS LEFT EAR HEARING AID (ICD-389.9)
DIABETES INSULIN DEP CONTROLLED (ICD-250.01)
Hx of CATARACT (ICD-366.9)
HYPERTENSION, BENIGN (ICD-401.1)
CONJUNCTIVITIS, CHRONIC (ICD-372.00)
PRESBYOPIA (ICD-367.4)
POSTTRAUMATIC STRESS DISORDER (A1) (DS4-309.81)

Current Medications:
LESCOL CAPS 40 MG 1 tab po hs
HUMULIN 70/30 SUSP 70-30 % 52 units sc in am, 35 units sc in pm
LOTENSIN TABS 10 MG 1 tab po q day x 90 days stop date 8/14/01
MULTIVITAMINS TABS 1 tab po q day x 6 months stop date 11/14/01
ASPIRIN TABS 325 MG Take1 tab po qd

A prison listing of List's medical problems including Post Transmatic
Stress Disorder.

JOHN E LIST   Inmate Housing Location: New Jersey State Prison-Main
Male DOB: 09/17/1925   SBI #: 000308038A   Booking #: 226472

03/30/2001 - Internal Correspondence: Added diagnosis of PTSD to problem list
Provider: Arthur D. Boxer, MD
Location of Care: New Jersey State Prison
This document contains confidential information

Chart Note

Narrative:

Problems/Allergies/Observation Changes

Problems:
Added new problem of POSTTRAUMATIC STRESS DISORDER (A1) (DS4-309.81)
Assessed POSTTRAUMATIC STRESS DISORDER (A1) as improved

List's Post Transmatic Stress Disorder diagnosis.

C 10 138 858
List , John E

Why Have We Withheld Benefits?

We have withheld benefits because you are currently incarcerated at Trenton State Prison for a felony. Veterans who are rated 20 percent or less are only entitled to half of the rate of compensation. Therefore we have withheld half of the compensation that you were originally entitled for the period during which you have been incarcerated.

What Did We Decide?

We determined that the following condition(s) was/were related to your military service, so service connection has been granted:

Medical Description	Percent (%) Assigned	Effective Date
Post traumatic stress disorder	10%	Feb 15, 2003

ℛ 10-27-05

OCT 2 4 2005

JOHN E LIST
TRENTON STATE PRISON
PN #226472
SB1 308038A
TRENTON NJ 08625

In Reply Refer To: 309/21/cp
C 10 138 858
LIST , John E

Dear Mr. List :

We made a decision on your notice of disagreement received on May 28, 2004.

This letter tells you about your entitlement amount and payment start date and what we decided. It includes a copy of our rating decision that gives the evidence used and reasons for our decision. We have also included information about additional benefits, what to do if you disagree with our decision, and who to contact if you have questions or need assistance.

What Is Your Entitlement Amount And Payment Start Date?

Your monthly entitlement amount is shown below:

Total Award Amount	Amount Withheld	Monthly Entitlement Amount	Payment Start Date	Reason For Change
$104.00	$52.00	$52.00	Mar 1, 2003	Entitlement to compensation at the 10% rate, withholding due to incarceration
106.00	53.00	53.00	Dec 1, 2003	Cost of living adjustment, withholding continues
108.00	54.00	54.00	Dec 1, 2004	Cost of living adjustment, withholding continues

Department of Veterans Affairs Certification of Compensation
entitlement for Post Transmatic Stress Disorder ($54 per month)
effective February 15, 2003.

6

The Murders

It happened before the Columbine school massacre, before the bombing of the Federal Building and its nursery in Oklahoma City, before the murder of eight infants by a woman who was never charged with a crime because her help was needed for research on infanticide, and before Andrea Yates drowned her five kids in a bathtub.

On November 9, 1971, in the city of Westfield, New Jersey, I, John List, age 46, shot and killed my wife, Helen, 47; my mother, Alma, 84; and my three children: Patricia Marie, 16; John Frederick, 15; and Frederick Michael, 13.

I wish I had never done what I did. I've regretted my action and prayed for forgiveness ever since. But at the time it seemed the only way out of what appeared to me to be a situation of utter hopelessness both for me and for my family. Over a period of six months my options had dwindled and finally vanished into the black emptiness at the bottom of the mine shaft of my life.

For several weeks prior to my murders I deliberated in a seemingly rational way what I should do to resolve my problems. In the evenings I sat in my recliner chair in the second parlor between the front parlor and the ballroom of our too-expensive mansion and I prayed intently. Unlike formal prayers in church, my meditations took the form of conversations with God, the only entity in whom I felt I could confide. Contrary to what has been written about my murders, religious thoughts were actually peripheral to my deliberation of what had to be done. My thoughts focused mainly on my failure to provide for my family coupled with my desire to ease their suffering from our collapsed financial situation. If my profound religious faith entered the picture in the sense of providing an explanation, or in some way a justification for my actions, this has to be seen as evidence of the muddled state of my mind.

Nonetheless, given my religious upbringing and involvement it was natural that my lonely conversations would be held in the context of my religious faith. Thus, my whispered petition went something like this: "Dear heavenly father, I pray to you in the name of Jesus Christ our Savior. You know our needs. Helen is continually ill, and we don't seem to be able to get any help to cure her. Please allow her to get well. We need her to be both a mother and a wife. I am trying as hard as I can to provide a living for us. But somehow I don't have your blessing to succeed in this effort. We have so many bills that are past due and I don't see how we can keep the family going much longer. If I just abandon my family that would be traumatic especially for the children, but also for Helen and Mother. Helen would never be able to take care of the children, especially without any income. And it would be unfair to Mother to dump this situation into her lap, especially at her age. But what else could or should I do?"\

With the systematic and logical method of a trained accountant, I proceeded to consider and evaluate all of the alternative courses of action available to me. "Dear God," I asked, "what should I do?" If I were to commit suicide (considering this mortal sin for the first time in my life), I was certain that I could never get to Heaven. And I definitely wanted all of us to be reunited there.

But if I remained down and out in Westfield, NJ, it would be difficult to get any kind of relief for the family from social services, or so I thought. (I thought that a family could not receive financial help if the father was present.) In any case, I felt that the family would suffer a permanently destructive, traumatic blow. The more I considered alternative courses of action and their consequences, the more I feared what would result from our financial and economic ruin. In retrospect, I realize that this fear undoubtedly grew out of excessive pride on my part.

My prayerful evaluation of alternative courses of action went like this: If I kill only Helen, because of her inability to help the rest of the family, I will cause an awful burden to fall on the children. It would scar them for life and might well drive them away from church. This would be unacceptable.

I know that it is wrong to kill, I admitted in my prayer, except in cases of self-preservation, and this is not such a situation. Also, if I deliberately kill, can I be forgiven for sinning in such a deliberate manner? Eventually, I concluded that I could be forgiven if I sincerely repented and lived a life that would not cause any more harm to others. To what extent was this rationalization? Had I already made up my mind what I was going to do and only sought some justification for going through with it? I really can't answer that question, even thirty-five years after the murders.

One thing is certain. During more than three weeks of preparation for the coming tragedy, I wrestled with some pretty heavy questions of values and morality. With the rest of the family in bed, the lonely man in my body sat and considered his options while seated in a recliner chair next to the ballroom where the corpses would be laid out. As I considered and rejected non-violent alternatives solutions to my hopeless situation, I got the feeling that I was simply drilling a circular hole making a deeper erut at each turn. This downward spiral led to the rejection of all options except that offered by murder. Could it be that my obsessive-compulsive personality disorder played a role in this reasoning? Or is it possible that my post traumatic stress disorder (PTSD) stemming from World War II combat influenced my fateful decision? (NOTE: The magistrate who presided at my trial and appeal held that my inability to recall details of combat ruled out any PTSD effect. Psychiatrists have determined, however, that inability to recall details of traumatic stress is in itself a hallmark symptom of the disorder.)

I have to believe that these mental impairments might have at least supplied momentum to my decision, rendered it finally, fatally irreversible. I also believe that the acquisition of a lethal weapon and making preparations for the establishment of a new identity contributed to the reinforcement of motivation to carry out my terrible scheme. At first I had forgotten that I already had in the house two pistols: a 9 mm Austrian Styre pistol I bought from a rear echelon G.I. in France at the end of the war, and an old .22 caliber pistol that had belonged to my father. (Mother had brought the .22 with her household effects when she moved to Westfield on the invitation of my wife, and probably gave it to me for safekeeping.)

The option of getting a stranger to purchase a gun for me was ruled out, because I couldn't be certain that the person might be either an undercover police officer or someone who might turn me in for their own personal advantage.

I had first tried to get around the New Jersey law that required a permit to purchase a handgun by picking one up in a state where none was required. The most convenient location was Delaware. So I drove there to get a pistol but found out that I could only do so if I had a Delaware driver's license. I then went to Plan B and on October 11, 1991, I filled out an applicadtion for a permit to buy a pistol, which I claimed to need for self defense, in Westfield. I seem to recall that I gave the names of the Lutheran school principal and Pastor Rehwinkel as character references.

After a week or so, I called the police station to ask about my permit and was told that it had not yet been authorized. By then my decision to resolve my career and family problems had taken control, had spawned an overriding compulsion to act. In a hurry, I didn't even have time to wait for the gun permit and concentrated on finding the pistols that had to be somewhere in the house. I rummaged through boxes of discarded household effects in a storage room and found the weapons. I remember how excited I was to find them. It was like finding buried treasure.

Unfortunately, there was no 9 mm ammunition for the Steyr and only decades old bullets for the .22, and I was not about to rely on such old ammo for my *mission*. So I went to a gun store and purchased fresh ammunition. I then test fired the pistols at a firing range. In the Army I had scored an Expert rating with the standard Colt .45, and I found that I could still fire the pistols accurately 25 years after the war.

In preparing for the coming tragedy, I also obtained several Social Security cards to backstop four different aliases. This was easier than I had thought it would be. I just went to different Social Security offices, where I filled out applications using different names, dates and places of birth. The cards were issued the same day. I don't know if this resulted from lax procedures or a subjective decision stemming from my appearance. I dressed neatly, was always well-groomed and probably projected an image of rather nerdy innocence. As it turned out I didn't need these cards for my travel to Denver, whee I obtained one by mail from Washington DC in the name of Robert P. Clark that served to document my existence for the better part of the next 18 years.

Originally I had planned to murder my family on November 2nd, All Saints' Day in the church calendar, dedicated to commemorate the departed faithful. In my deranged state of mind, I must have thought that this date would provide my killing with some sort of religious sanction. In any case I re-scheduled the operative date to November 9th, probably to fit with the children's schedule.

Although the conservative Missouri Synod of thc Lutheran Church served, and still serves, as the centerpiece of my spiritual life, I don't believe in the use of my faith as a moral crutch to justify my misdeeds. In fact, my using my belief in God's forgiveness of our sins as a factor in planning what I knew to be a sinful resolution of our hopeless situation, was proof of what I now regard as my deranged state of mind.

In this context I have to note my resentment with the manner in which media coverage of my life has overplayed the role of my religious faith in my life. This misconception was a major theme in the 1993 CBCS TV movie *Judgment Day: The John List Story*, starring Robert Blake. Ironically, Blake was later charged with murdering his wife. Acquitted in criminal court, Blake was found guilty in a civil action.

November 9, 1971: My Day of Infamy

It started like any other day. I made the kids' breakfast, got them off to school and washed the dishes. My wife, Helen, appeared as usual in her bathrobe, poured herself a copy of coffee and sat down at the kitchen table to eat a piece of toast and look at the morning newspaper. I went out to the garage to retrieve the pistols, which I put in the large side pockets of my old green Army field jacket. Before returning to the houise I quickly reviewed in my mind what I was about to do. I knew that once started, there could be no turning back. I would have to kill each and every member of the family, since it would be unspeakably painful for any one of them to have to live with the knowledge of what had happened. Given their young ages, it would have been especially painful for the children. I was also given pause by the fact that I had never before killed anyone at close range. If any German soldier or civilian had been killed by my 60 mm mortar during combat in WW II that was different. That was something one might call *collateral damage*. Nothing personal.

I took a deep breath, walked into the kitchen with my hand on the cold grip of the Styre, moved up behind my wife, pulled the pistol out and fired into the back of her head for instant effect. I stepped back as her disease-ravaged and now dead body slid silently, sort of in slow motion, to the floor. I put the pistol back-ing my jacket pocket and checked to make sure that all of the doors were securely locked before I purposefully walked up the stairs to the third floor apartment of my mother.

She was eating breakfast and got up to greet me "good morning" and a kiss when mindful of my mission, I felt like Judas Iscariot must have felt when he kissed Jesus Christ. Mother immediately asked me what the loud noise was that she had heard from downstairs. I told her I ididn't know what it was, but tha was why I had come upstairs to see if I could see anything from her windows, which overlooked the backyard. I asked her to take a look out her sitting room windows while I looked out her kitchen window. As she proceeded through the door to the attic, I shot her from behind. I tried to move her to her bed, but she was too heavy and I had to leave her on the floor.

I then returned to the first floor and moved Helen into the ballroom. I found two sleeping bags, placed Helen on one of them, and later would put the children down beside her. Then I returned to the kitchen to clean up. I was amazed at the amount of blood there. I had to clean it up as best I cold so that the children would not see it and be shocked and stressed out by the sight. I had to mop the floor three or four times, and, because we had no mop-wringer, I had to wring accumulated blood out of the mop by hand. Was this a gruesome task? Yes, of course it was. But nothing could stay me from what I had to do.

Afterward, I had lunch. When she interviewed me on ABC's 20/20 Downtown program (on Feb 20, 2002) Connie Chung asked me how I could eat lunch after murdering my wife and mother, I answered that "I was hungry." I realize that this gave the strong impression of my being mercilessly cold-blooded. But given a few moments to reflect on the question, I would have added that I was conditioned during my years in the infantry, especially during combat, to eat whenever and wherever I had the opportunity. It's a primary, overriding concern having to do with survival, which I suppose is made more acute by the special stress of military life. Like sleeping whenever there was an opportunity to make up for lost sleep or to store energy for lost sleep yet to come. How else can you explain the phenomenon of actually catching a few seconds (minutes?) of sleep during a night march? Ask any G.I. active duty or veteran.

After lunch, I called Burt Goldstein's office to tell him that I wouldn't be in touch with the office because we had to travel to North Carolina because of the illness of Helen's mother. Burt had moved his office to Long Island in partnership with another insurance agent whom he knew and respected. The new group would expand their business to include financial planning services and the sale of securities as well as insurance policies. Since it was not necessary for me to work in that office, Burt had loaned me a desk, chair and two file cabinets for my home office in the first sitting room.

Knowing that my income from insurance work was nil, Burt had on his own initiative loaned me $500. As noted in my confession letter, I hoped that the $1,000 insurance coverage I wrote on each member of my family would repay this debft and cover burial expenses. Much later I found out that the insurance company found that the policies had lapsed because the premiums had not been paid.

After my call to Burt's office in the late morning or early afternoon, I drove downtown to the bank. I first cashed a check at the drive-through window, parked the car, and entered the bank. Then I cashed another personal check, which may have just about overdrawn my account. I then went to a safety deposit box that was in my mother's and my names. Mother had stored several U.S. Savings Bonds there, some in her name with me as beneficiary and some held jointly. I took those held jointly and cashed them, telling the cashier that Mother was going on a trip and needed the cash. I even asked the cashier to compute the amount of interest included in the refund for income tax purposes. I left the bank with about $2,000 in cash. (I should mention that I never withdrew funds from

Mother's bank account without her permission, as some fiction writers have claimed. Every time I asked for financial help, she made out a check in my name and signed it.)

After my transactions at the bank, I returned home and prepared for the next phase of my murderous actions: killing my children. I experienced no qualms or feelings of remorse, only what might be described as an elevated level of consciousness as I moved on to implement an action plan that had developed an irreversible momentum of its own. It was like I was on some sort of cruise control and had no choice but to finish what I had started.

Pat and Fred had part-time jobs after school in downtown Westfield. On this D-Day, Pat felt poorly and didn't go to work. I picked her up at school, and I may have picked up some neighbor kids and driven them home as well. As we walked from the laundry room into the kitchen, I shot Pat, moved her into the ballroom and cleaned up the blood.

Next I picked up Fred at his work place, drove him home and shot him in the same manner that I'd shot Pat.

Afterwards, I picked up John, who had been playing in a soccer game. I shot him in the same place and manner I had shot his siblings. The only difference was that after I shot my namesake, his body twitched in convulsions. Seeing this, which had not occurred with any of my other victims, I must have panicked, because I emptied the Styre and some of the .22 bullets into John. As with the other victims, I had attempted to kill John in a way that would not cause him to suffer. Some writers claimed that John had consciously tried to fight me. This is but one of many examples appearing in books about me in which outside observers have made assumptions of events without direct knowledge of them. I am sure that John was killed by the first shot and that his body movements were only muscular reflexes operating in some automatic manner. In any case, the tragedy was finished. I had murdered five members of my family, but in my mind it was a single act rather than five separate murders, which the court held as the basis for imposing five consecutive life terms.

After a final cleanup of blood, I went into the ballroom where the bodies were laid out and prayed for the family. I did not do this on my knees as portrayed in the made-for-TV movie about my crime. Standing with my head bowed, I prayed these words: "Dear Heavenly Father, I pray to you in the name of Jesus our savior. Please take the family into your heavenly home. They are all so innocent in this matter." I then recited the Lord's Prayer.

I felt spent, sated. Something like the empty feeling left after sex. I went into the second parlor to write my confession letter to Pastor Rehwinkel (see below), and shorter notes of confession to some of my relatives and Helen's sister, Jean Syffert.

Demonstrating the same diligence in tidying up that had made me a model soldier during quarters' inspections in the Army, I carefully and thoroughly cleaned the pistols while they were still warm. I then placed the weapons together with unused ammunition on the floor next to the filing cabinet where I had carefully placed my letter of confession, final arrangements instructions and letters to be mailed. The object of leaving the weapons in the open was to convince the police that wherever I was, I was no longer armed. It surprised me, therefore, when I saw newspaper articles in Colorado that described fugitive John List as "armed and dangerous."

I turned the lights down and telephoned our neighbors, the Baeders, whose daughter was a close friend of Pat, to tell them that the children would not be going to school for a while, as they had flown to North Carolina with their mother to be with Helen's sick mother. I lied that I was to drive down to join them the next day.

I then packed for my departure a few clothes, some books and some of the combat simulation games I'd bought over the years. I seem to recall that I ended up with a suitcase, an overnight bag and two or three boxes of books and games. I don't recall taking any pictures of the family. (I pictures I have in prison were sent to me by my cousin Ralph List. Somehow these had ended up in Aunt Lydia's house in Frankenmuth, Michigan.)

I've been asked what became of Tinker Bell, a little Pekinese dog that the kids loved and I tolerated. I recall that I let her out of the house early in the morning and thought no more about her. She simply never returned. It might have been that the family pet somehow sensed the impending tragedy and fled to parts unknown.

My Confession Letter

Dear Pastor Rehwinkel:

I know that what has been done is wrong from all that I have been taught and that any reasons that I might give will not make it right. But you are the one person that I know that, while not condoning this will at least possibly understand why I felt that I had to do this.

1. I wasn't earning anywhere near enough to support us. Everything I tried seemed to fall to pieces. True, we could have gone bankrupt and maybe gone on welfare.

2. But that brings me to my next point. Knowing the type of location that one would have to live in plus dthe environment for the children plus the effect on them knowing they were on welfare was just more than I thought they could & should endure. I know that they were willing to cut back but this involved a lot more than that.

3. With Pat being so determined to get into acting I was also fearful as to what this might do to her continuing to be a Christian. I'm sure it wouldn't have helped.

4. Also, with Helen not going to church I knew that this would harm the children eventually in their attendance. I had continued to hope that she would begin to come to church soon. But when I mentioned to her that Mr. Jutzi wanted to pay her an Elders call. She just blew up and stated that she wanted her name taken off the church rolls. Again this could only have given an adverse result for the children's continued attendance.

So that is the sum of it. If any one of these had been the [only] condition we might have pulled through but this was just too much. At least I'm certain that all have gone to heaven now. If things had gone on, who knows if that would be the case.

Of course Mother got involved because doing what I did to my family would have been a tremendous shock to her at her age. Therefore, knowing that she is also a Christian I felt it best that she be relieved of the troubles of this world that would have hit her.

After it was all over I said some prayers for them all—from the hymn book. That was the least that I could do. Now for the final arrangements: Helen and the children have all agreed that they would prefer to be cremated. Please see to it that the costs are kept low.

For Mother, she has a plot at the Frankenmuth Church cemetery. Please contact Mr. Herman Schellhas, Rr 4, Vasar, Mich 41768. He's married to a niece of Mother's & knows what arrangements are to be made. She always wanted Rev.Herman Zehnder to preach the sermon, but he's not well.

Also I'm leaving some letters in your care. Please send them on and add whatever comments you think appropriate.

The relationships are as follows:

Mrs. Lydia Meyer—Mother's sister

Mrs. Eva Morris—Helen's mother

Jean Syfert—Helen's sister.

Also I don't know what will happen to the books & other personal things. But to the extent possible I'd like them to be distributed as you see fit. Some books might go into the school or church library.

Originally I had planned this for Nov 1—All Saints Day. But travel arrangements were delayed. I thought it would be an appropriate day for them to get to heaven. As for me, please let me be dropped from the congregation rolls. I leave myself in the hands of Gods Justice and Mercy. I don't doubt that He is able to help us, but apparently he saw fit not to answer my prayers any way I had hoped that they would be answered. This makes me think that perhaps it was for the best as far as children's souls are concerned. I know that many will only look at the additional years that they could have lived but if finally they were no longer Christians what would be gained.

Also I'm sure many will say "How could anyone do such a horrible thing?" My only answer is it isn't easy and was only done after much thought. One other thing. It may seem cowardly to have always shot from behind, but I didn't want any of them to know even at the last second that I had to this to them.

John got hurt more because he seemed to struggle longer. The rest were immediately out of pain. John didn't consciously feel anything either.

Please remember me in your prayers. I will need them, whether or not the government does its duty as it sees fit. I'm only concerned with making my peace with God & of this I am assured because of Christ dying even for me.

P.S. Mother is in the hallway in the attic—3rd floor. She was too heavy to move.

[signed] John"

7

Fast Forward Into a New Life

As the place where I wanted to resettle after the murders I had in mind the area of Denver, Colorado, where the mountains had appealed to me since childhood. I had no specific plans on how to get there, however, and it may have been this absence of a travel plan that facilitated my evasion of a national manhunt initiated by the FBI after the discovery of my crime by the Westfield police aided by a high school drama teacher a month after the murders.

The absence of a detailed escape scenario may have grown out of a deliberate decision to maintain flexibility in my actions, though this seems unlikely for a person with my obsessive—compulsive personality. It seems more likely that the ad hoc nature of my escape was produced by a fatalistic resignation to my fate. I had absolutely expected to be caught by law enforcement officers within a day or two, a week at the outside. The expectation of my imminent arrest and death by execution (capital punishment was on the books in those days) must have produced in me a sort of fatalistic peace of mind. I was freed from worry by certain knowledge of my imminent physical demise. Could it be that what makes people worry is uncertainty, fear of what could happen or might happen? In my case I knew, or thought I knew, what would happen and this put me on a sort of mentally relaxed cruise control as I moved into my new life.

However, during the nearly twenty-four hours that elapsed between the murders and my leaving the scene of the crime I acted in a deliberate manner. After all, I wasn't going to do the work of the police for them.

Ordering indefinite suspension of milk and mail deliveries didn't require much imagination. Such actions required no explanations. I needed a cover story, however, to explain the absence of my entire family to schools and employers. That's why I devised the story about having to travel to North Carolina to visit Helen's ailing mother. I used this to cover the children's absence from school. On my way out of town the morning after the murders I dropped off a note with the same story at the insurance agency office in Westfield where Pat and Fred worked.

I burned my passport (together with photos and movies) to leave the impression with investigators that I had left the country. Leaving my car in a long-term parking lot at Kennedy International Airport was intended to substantiate this fiction.

In the course of my final house inspection, which I did with a clear mind and deliberate purpose, I came across some family snapshots. I tore off my image from these pictures and incinerated them together with other documentation of my former life, to reduce the risk of these photos being reproduced in newspapers or used by the police on "wanted" posters. I was surprised about a month later to see a newspaper article with my picture in it. This must have been a photo that appeared in a local newspaper article that announced my arrival in town when I took a position at the Jersey City bank.

By the time of my trial, I was sorry that I hadn't disassembled the guns and put their parts together with unused ammo in several trash cans like those found in rest areas along interstate highways.

I disposed of my house keys by mailing them to my home address in a stamped envelope.

More than thirty years after my final, desperate solution to my family problems, I can still reconstruct my largely improvised escape to a new life in the West. I should mention that I had with the aid of an atlas, considered a number of alternative destinations. In addition to Denver, I considered Phoenix and smaller towns in Arizona as well as the San Francisco area. I had read somewhere that people who had committed crimes often fled to the other side of the country. This ruled out San Francisco, which was also spotlighted by an asocial invasion of "hippies." Since Arizona could get terribly hot, that left Denver as my best destination.

On the morning after the murders I woke up early, having slept fitfully, which I guess was to be expected. Before leaving the house, a mansion that had played a large role in my undoing, and after burning documents in the Weber grill, I turned the radio to a classical music station before making a final visit to the bodies laid out on the floor there.

I then loaded the car and departed. First I drove to an expressway, headed in a southerly direction and stopped in a small town where there was a Railway Express (RE) office. I sent the pre-packed boxes of books and war games to the RE office in Fort Wayne, Indiana. I then headed to New York City and placed my bags in a luggage storage box in the central bus terminal. I then drove out to

John F. Kennedy International Airport on Long Island. There I followed signs to a self-parking lot, drove to the top level and left the car.

Before leaving, I placed my driver's license, several other pieces of identification (without photos) and the car keys in the ashtray. I then walked back to the terminal and took a bus into the city. During this ride I deliberated my next move and finally decided to take the train to Philadelphia. After retrieving my bags, I took a cab to the Penn Station, which is right across the street from where I had worked for the American Photography Corporation.

The train pulled out at about 5:30 p.m. and crossed the Hudson River into New Jersey. I was a bit concerned that I might meet someone that I knew who might be commuting to his home. Once we got past the Westfield area I breathed easier. From the Philadelphia RR Station, I took a cab to the Greyhound Bus Station where I boarded a bus to Detroit and from there to Jackson (Michigan). I realized it was unlikely that I would meet anyone I knew in Detroit; it would be even less likely in Jackson. I got a room in a motel on the pedestrian mall downtown and took a nap.

According to my recollection, aided by my Perpetual Calendar, this is the path and timing of my travel into a fresh start.

Tuesday, November 9th 1971—the killings
Wednesday November 10th—left Westfield
Thursday November 11th—arrived in Jackson, MI
November 15th or 16th—to Ft. Wayne, IN by bus
Thursday November 18th—left Ft. Wayne by bus
Friday, November 19—left Galesburg, IL by train
Saturday, November 20th—arrived Denver.

When I shipped my boxes in NJ, I was told that it might take five days for them to get to Fort Wayne. This slow speed of the new AMTRAK service controlled the speed of my cross-country travel.

I arrived in Denver in the late morning. It was a clear, cold day. There was no snow left from the big storm that hit the area in early September. I walked up to the central part of downtown to buy a map of the city and check in at a hotel.

Before leaving Westfield, I had purchased a money belt like the one I had used in the army for the secure storage of extra cash. I used this portable bank for weeks until I established a regular bank account in Golden, CO.

For identification, I used the various names that appeared on my Social Security cards—one use for each—until I used them up. Finally I decided on the name Robert "Bob" Peter Clark, for which I had to obtain a new card. (Later I wished that I'd chosen "Paul" for a middle name, but I normally used only the initial "P" anyway.) To document my new, "full time" identity, which I would need to get decent employment, open a bank account and eventually to obtain a driver's license, I needed only to write a letter to the Social Security Administration in Washington DC. I explained that I had lost my card and needed to get a duplicate. I gave as my birth date April 26, 1930, which made me about four and a half years younger than my actual age.

Later, when I needed to apply for a driver's license, a friend advised me to obtain a Social Security card that would be better backstopped than the one I had obtained as a "lost" card duplicate. The idea was to use the actual birth date of a real person named Clark who had died at an early age. I spent many hours in the Denver Library scanning microfilm files and finally found a Clark, Richard. This would have been a good fit and would have provided better protection against an investigation (e.g., by the IRS) revealing my SSN identity as bogus. I finally decided to stay with my admittedly thin alias identification, mainly because I had used the name "Bob" so much that I would have had a problem switching to "Richard" or "Dick" as my first name. Henceforth, I simply made sure to pay my income tax in full and on time to minimize the chance of becoming the subject of an IRS audit.

Apart from my temporary concern over the strength of my alias to survive a serious review, my transition from John E. List to Robert P. Clark went smoothly.

Born again? Well, yes, in a way.

Analysis of My Handwriting

Handwriting analysis (Graphology) is a tool for personality assessment widely used by employment agencies and employers seeking insights into the strengths and weaknesses of prospective or current employee s. The Central Intelligence Agency makes use of graphology as a tool in creating personality profiles. My Army platoon mate Austin "Red" Goodrich, who served as a CIA case officer, called on a noted handwriting analyst (Mark Hopper of the Handwriting Research Corp.) to review several samples of my handwriting collected over a ten-year period (1990-2000). All of the writing was subject neutral (e.g., the text of the Mayflower Compact) and none of the samples provided any hint of the writer's [my] identity.

Hopper found that the handwriting samples strongly suggested a writer who was very intelligent, analytical, disciplined, curious, careful, conscientious and cautious—all attractive qualities for employment. At the same time, Hopper noted that the writer might not last long on the job because of poor social skills, including problems with building relationships, teaching/communicating and activities requiring people skills. The analysis also strongly suggested a low level of social tolerance and a high level of emotional aggression, anger and instability. An extremely high propensity to jealousy, introversion and secretiveness were also identified by the analyst, who concluded that: "Subject is the kind of person who would like to live in an apartment by himself."

The handwriting analyst also concluded that my writing strongly suggested the need for psychiatric intervention. (n.b. Psychiatrists who diagnosed my post traumatic stress disorder made the same recommendation.)

8

Born Again—Sort of

On Sunday, November 21, 1971, I missed attending a church service for the first time I could remember. Instead I took a long walk west on Colfax (US 40), the main east-west street in Denver. It was a clear, cool day and the mountains provided a majestic backdrop to the scene. I must have walked four or five miles and despite my lack of exercise in recent months the expected aches and pains never appeared. I slept well in John served in the same platoon with me in Germany and the Philippines in WW II. my motel that night.

During the next few days I took a bus to the downtown area just to look around. I wore an old gray twill overcoat, which was nondescript and warm enough, but I needed some head gear unlike my past snap-brim hats. I bought a black synthetic leather cap with a short visor that I pulled well forward to partially conceal my facial features. Although my story wouldn't hit the Rocky Mountain News for several days, I thought it better to be safe than sorry. So I avoided getting into the view of police on foot, in coffee shops or in squad cars. But when I came across them, I deliberately looked them straight in the eye in to avoid the appearance of a fugitive.

I immediately looked in the newspaper want ads for jobs. The first one I applied for was at the International House of Pancakes, where they needed a "fast short order cook." I applied in the morning and was told to report for work in the afternoon. It soon became apparent to my employers and me that I didn't fit into this particular slot. I then went to an employment agency and got two leads. After one came up empty, my case worker met me and drove me to a job vacancy in west Denver.

She was impressed that I was willing to look for work on such a cold, snowy day. She introduced me to the chef at the Holiday Inn, Jess Plunk, who hired me as a grill cook, and I reported for work the following afternoon.

There was one big problem. I didn't have a Social Security card. Fortunately, I had written to the Social Security office in Washington some days before to request a replacement for the card I, Robert P. Clark, had lost. Luckily the replacement card arrived just before the end of the year when Holiday Inn would have to submit their employment report to the Feds. The next day the lady from the employment agency came by my motel to collect her fee, which I paid in cash. She mentioned that she and her husband planned to move, and I wondered if she intended to give my payment to the agency or simply keep it for herself. Was I getting cynical?

I took a cab to a motel directly behind the Holiday Inn and signed in there. I bought a newspaper and found on an inside page a photo of myself that appeared in an ardtricle desxcribing what had been discovered at 421 Hillside Ave, Westfield, NJ. The article said that the police were looking for me but I was wanted only *for questioning*. Yeah right. Just then, as I left my room for work, I noticed two police cars parked behind the Holiday Inn facing in opposite directions to let the drivers converse through their open front windows. I might have naturally assumed that they were there to pick me up for questioning, in which case I might have fled the scene. But my fatalistic inertia kicked in. I walked as far away from the patrol cars as possible, turned down the brim of my cap, and avoided looking directly at them as I walked purposefully into the motel kitchen where I confronted a more immediate problem.

What should I do with the white cook's clothes that were handed to me? I had to ask the young Hispanic wwho had given me a lift back to Denver whether I should wear the whites over my street clothes or strip down and wear only the new clothes. That was a stupid question, but apparently Jess Plunk was willing to forgive a little stupidity if dthe new guy showed up on time and sober, unlike his predecessors, who often showed up tardy or drunk or both.

I felt that the danger of being recognized by the police was at least matched by getting recognized from the photo in the newspaper by my co-workers or guests at the motel. This risk was reduced by the difference between how I looked in the press photo and how I appeared in real life. In the photo I was clean shaven and wore a suit and tie. In my new incarnation I wore a sports shirt and had cultivated a small moustache. So far, so good, I thought.

The worst shock I got during my work at Holiday Inn was when I new hostess was brought in to meet the kitchen staff. An electrical shock coursed through my body as I looked at the woman—a younger version of Helen.

I soon realized that I wouldn't be able to afford living in a motel for long, so I checked out a couple of trailer parks in the area. I'd been told by a woman who prepared food in the kitchen that there was a trailer for rent at the smaller park. It was an older model 8' by 30' that needed a thorough cleaning because the owner had owned two dogs with limited toilet training. However, the unit had a built-in bed, fridge, stove and possibly a table and chairs. And the price was rightr! For $1,500 it was all mine. Of course, a few problems came at no charge: a leaking water pipe, a worn-out electric pipe tape and cracked window caulking. All could be fixed before winter reappeared. I kept the thermostat at a constant 60 degrees.

After I got my Social Security card and a few paychecks, I decided it was time to open a checking account. I still had my money belt for the secure transportation of cash, but that outmoded and rather uncomfortable. So I went to a bank in downtown Golden, CO, about four miles away. The teller asked me where I had my previous account and I told her that I had not had one. The only identification I had was my Social Seckkurity card, which is not supposed to be used for identification, but my polite, humble manner got me a checking account.

About a year later, Jess got sick and was replaced by a series of cooks whose tenure was shortened by their addiction to John Barleycorn. Eventually, a fine man named Gary Morrison wa hired as chef, and he promptly appointed me to be head cook on the serving line. I had prepared for this modest move up my professional cooking ladder by closely observing the line. I could handle broiling steaks in the way I had grilled steaks on my charcoal grill, and I already knew how to slice the prime rib, which I did when the chef wasn't available.

At about this time I met an easy-going, friendly man named Bob Wetmore, who did the heavy-duty duty cleaning in the restaurant and we became good friends. Bob had graduated *cum lauda* from the school of hard knocks, had worked laying rails as a gandy dancer, roped steers and lived in hobo jungles. Ill treatment at the hands of his family had driven Bob from the Lutheran church and his close association with a Japanese family had brought him to Buddhism. He once took me to a temple where he and his friends worshipped.

Some months after I arrived, Gary Morrison left Holiday Inn to take a position as chef at the Pinery, an upscale housing development vuilt around a golf course of the same name odn the south side of Denver. Gary was born in Sarnia, Ontario, across the river from Port Huron. Later his family moved to Calgary, Alberta, and he received his chef's training at the Canadian Railways culinary school, which he told me had a standing equivalent to the Cordon Bleu school in Paris. I could tell he had good training and enjoyed his career.

In a short time, Gary offered me the job of assistant or *sous chef* at the Pinery and I jumped at the opportunity of working with Gary in a position that paid more than I had been making. My new job required me to move from Golden to Denver, where I was able to find a small apartment near the University of Denver. My apartment had a small kitchen off the dining/living room area, plus a bedroom and bath. In the morning I walked towards his apartment complex, and sometimes he would pick m up before I got there and we'd drive together to work.

We had plenty of time to talk, in the course of which we developed a close friendship. Gary told me how he played ice hockey, and joked about how he and his friends had tried to drink "Canada Dry." I never really noticed that Gary drank a lot. But once, when his wife Sharon drove me home after Gary left work early, I mentioned that Gary had said he had drunk more than usual because it was his birthday. She responded that that was his third birthday of that month. I began to think that hitting the hard stuff might be an occupational hazard for professional cooks. I had a dim recollection of how our Co K cooks drank whiskey we suspected was supplied to them by officers as a trade off for the prime steaks they feasted on in the mess hall kitchen late at night.

In January, 1973, a bump appeared in the road of Bob Clark's life, when Gary told me he'd have to let me go, because there wasn't enough business at the Pinery restaurant to keep me on full time. He was sincerely sorry. Fortunately, I quickly got a job in the restaurant at The Denver, the city's leading department store. I worked there from 6:00a.m. to 1:30 p.m. with Sundays off. This gave me an opportunity to get back into religion, which had always played a central role in the life of John List.

While working at the Holiday Inn I wasn't able to go to church and had to nourish my spiritual needs by listening to two services broadcast over Denver radio stations. One was from a Missouri Synod congregation, the other from a Lutheran church of America congregation. I round that the LCA services weren't as radical as I had been led to believe in my childhood. I found out about a Creation Science group through the Missouri Synod broadcasts, and this led me to subscribe to a periodical that published articles by scientists that reconciled the differences between scientific and religious versions of creation. In addition to the biblical story of the creation of the Universe, these studies dealt with Noah's flood,dthe parting of the Red Sea, Joshua's asking the sun to stand still and other natural phenomena. I had previously read *The Flood* by Professor Rehwinkel, the father of my Pastor in Westfield, and other studies on this subject, which still fascinates me.

My intellectual curiosity was not limited to science and religion. I had read a booklet on how to win at roulette, and I bought a small roulette wheel to test its theory. It seemed there was some empirical evidence to support the theory, so I took short trips to Las Vegas and Reno to check it out. I had little financial suc-

cess, but Iwas able to limit my losses to my available means. At one casino, offi-
cials saw that I was using a system and they requested that I leave, which I did.

When I decided it was time to get back into attending church, the only question was which one. For reasons of security, I decided not to go to a Missouri
Synod Lutheran Church, where the chance of running into someone who knew
John List would be greater. I decided to go to an ALC church in downtown Denver, a couple of blocks from my bus line. At the time of my first visit, my suit was
at the cleaners, so I slipped into a rear pew wearing my old gray overcoat and a
rather tacky maroon sweater. For two Sundays I avoided meeting Pastor Robert
West by slipping out a side exit. Later I became a member of the Church by act
of affirmation, joined various committees and eventually was elected to the
Church Council as Treasurer.

My return to an active role in the church coincided with my easing back into
the professional career of my first life. Over the Labor Day weekend, I happened
to hear a TV ad for an H&R Block class on the preparation of income tax
returns. The classes were held at night at a location close to my bus line and I
signed up. Seated directly behind me was a fellow named Bob Miller, whose life
resembled my own. We were both graduates of Big Ten schools (he from the
University of Iowa), had worked in accounting and were both CPA's. Finally, we
both had crime in our past. Bob was on parole from a sentence imposed for bank
robbery. It seems that he had worked in a New York bank and may have been
laid off before he decided to go into business on his own. He said he started to
rob banks because of the way prisoners were mistreated and killed during the
Attica prison riots in upstate New York.

Bob was running a small accounting firm located in a former Catholic school
building where the Civilian Education and Training Administration (CETA) had
its offices. Bob had a young man and a woman working with him in his firm and
when the man left in February 1974, Bob offered the job to me. I had resigned
my job at The Denver to work at H.R. Block in hopes of earning ood money at
the height of the tax season. As it tuned out, that job fizzled for lack of new customers. (Old customers always wanted to work with the persons who had handled their returns previously.) In retrospect, I should have kept my day job at The
Denver and supplemented it with work in the moonlight at H&R Block. Live
and learn, as they say, but *they* probably weren't moving close to their forty-ninth
birthday as I was.

So Bob Miller's job offer, which paid more than what I had earned at The
Denver was opportune to say the least. It also might have ended my life as a fugitive had my employer been less discreet. The danger to my cover arose when Bob

said he would like to have me take over some of the contact work with his clients, but that I'd need a driver's license. When I said I wasn't sure I could get one, Bob elicited the story that I had killed my wife. I thought that he would keep the secret because he was an ex-con and no friend of the criminal justice system. I later learned that he had talked about me with the CETA manager, who had told him that he didn't need to know any more about my background. I lucked out again.

I spent more than a few hours at the library doing research to implement Bob's suggestion of backstopping a new legal identity with the name of an actual person deceased in childhood. Finally, I decided to go with what I had. I passed my driver's tests and got financing for a car in my adopted alias, a name authenticated by usage. I *was* Bob Clark. No other name would do.

I bought an orange VW, said to be the most noticeable and therefore safest color, with 50,000 miles on her. I put on an additional 80,000 miles, many of them navigating on scenic but treacherous mountain roads. I only needed to replace the engine and transmission.

In January 1975, an announcement was made at St. Pauls of a singles group was being formed art another ALC church, the largest in Denver. There were about a dozen participants. The group gathered for potluck meals and at church and members' homes, and took trips into the mountains. At one meeting we broke up into small discussion groups. A tall, attractive woman named Delores H. Miller was in my group. I liked the Christian views she expressed, though I could see she was under a great deal of stress. Her divorce from a military man had been finalized just a few weeks before. Several weeks later I got to know Delores better, and invited her out for supper on a Sunday night after a singles meeting. The plan was for me to pick Delores up at her residence which I had trouble finding. I had to call from a shopping center for directions and she seemed surprised that I showed up for our date. I'm sure that showed the stress she felt at the time.

We continued to date as our love matured during our courtship until we finally got married on November 23, 1985 in Baltimore County. The ceremony took place just a few miles from where I had married Helen 24 years before.

Meanwhile, I continued to change jobs and addresses the way a snake sheds its skin. Sometime in 1975, Bob, who considered me a partner, decided it was time to strike out on our own. Little did I know that by *striking out* he might have been thinking of the baseball term. We opened a small office in Wheat Ridge on the western side of Denver, and I moved into any apartment there. We still had some accounting contracts with small companies, but we never achieved our goal of making a lot of money during the tax season. It was agreed that I should get a fulltime day job and come in to help out evenings and on weekends. I got a job as Accountant and Chief Bookkeeper with the Roberto Distributing, whose president, Peter Roberto, was a wounded WWII veteran. He was also a congenial man who was pleasant to work with. To be closer to the job, I moved to Aurora on the east side of Denver. After several years, I decided to seek a more challenging position.

Meantime, Bob Miller had moved out west after selling his business to a man who cold make only a partial payment. When he returned a year later, the buyer was unable to produce payment of the balance, but did give Bob a partial payment, some of which Bob gave to me. After a brief visit with the younger of his two sons, Bob Miller ran out of money before he could visit his other son, who lived with his mother in Iowa. Bob pulled into a small roadside park and killed himself.

I was hired by American Packaging Co. (AAPC) in October, 1977. I supplemented my salary by working with H&R Block preparing income tax returns during my "free" time from 5:30 p.m. until the doors closed at 9:00 p.m. I also upgraded my credentials by taking an intensive course to prepare for the Enrolled Agent (EA) exam. An EA is permitted to represent a client at IRS hearings, and possibly, before the tax court. I passed all five parts of the exam on my first try, which I was told doesn't often happen.

After some years APC moved to a new plant in Aurora, which shortened my commute, and at about the same time I was able to do my tax work at a Block office near my home. One client drove all the way across town to have m do his taxes at my new location, which I took as a compliment.

Around 1980, three years after joining APC, the company bought an Apple II computer system, and I was assigned to procure the software needed to handle the company's accounting system. Generally it worked very well in producing financial reports, as well as our accounts receivable and accounts payable. I was able to make projections and allocations, which would have been very difficult to do manually. When the computer "crashed," as it did usually because of static electricity that built up on the plant floor, I had to transport the equipment for repair to a shop some 30 miles away. Fortunately the computer was small enough to pack into my orange VW Bug.

In April 1986 I was notified of my termination.

Apparently, my financial reports were executed too late to suit the firm's president. I was asked to help break in the next two controllers. The first of my successors lasted about six months. The second one left after about one year.

The time of this job loss was particularly unfortunate in that it came just a few months after Delores and I were married. Dee's family threw a nice party for us before we left on our honeymoon, which included stops for a swim at Virginia Beach and historical sightseeing at the restored colonial village in Williamsburg.

After I was fired at APC, I decided that it might be best to go into business on my own. My first thought was to operate an accounting and tax service, for which I was best qualified by my training and experience. However, I had learned from m experience with Bob Miller that it was extremely difficult to build up a clientele. So I canvassed a number of people to evaluate the benefit of obtaining leads to prospective clients through brokers. Those who had followed this route were not optimistic. They found that clients obtained in this way were unreliable heads of short-lived businesses, who had few or no funds to spend on accounting services.

I then looked into other business options made available through brokers handling franchises, but found the most attractive opportunity in a classified ad. With a modest investment, the would-be entrepreneur could purchase a franchise granting to sell coupon ads in a specific territory. The franchise holder would then sell enough ads to make up a small packet of coupons which would e printed and mailed out to addresses supplied by the franchise seller, who covered a large area. Of course, one had a number of fixed operating costs, including art work, printing, stuffing and sealing envelopes and postage. To shorten a long story of a business failure, suffice it to say that I lost money on each mailing and had to end the venture for lack of cash. Fortunately, the franchisee in Boulder softened the financial blow by purchasing my franchise at cost, less the amount I still owed on the purchase price.

I was back in the managerial unemployment line, represented in my job search by, among others, a headhunter firm in Richmond, Virginia. This led to a job in that city, which was the capital of the Confederacy and my last stop as a free man.

Reflecting on his experience with a loyal member of Saint Paul's Lutheran Church in Denver, Colorado, the Pastor, Rev. Robert A. West, DD, wrote: "I only know Bob Clark. I do not know John List."

…As a parish family our shock is not that a person like this could be in our midst, for we all have a hidden dark side in our lives, and the church is not a gallery for saints but a gathering place for sinners, but our shock is that the man we came to know and respect in his 11 years as our partner in ministry here at St.Paul's could have committed such a heinous act of violence against his family.

In a letter dated March 16, 1990, Rev. West wrote:

Dear Delores and Bob: Knowing that the trial is about to begin, I wanted each of you to know that you are in our thoughts and prayers here at St. Paul's. On Sunday, we will be praying for both of you with this prayer petition:

God of grace and mercy we offer a special prayer today for Bob and Delores as they prepare to face the trial of John List. Help them to cling to your promise given each of them in their baptism that you will never forsake them. Be a refuge and strength to them and to all whose lives have been touched by this tragedy....

9

The Jig's Up

Late in 1987, 16 years after the tragedy, I set forth on what turned out to be the final leg of my search for job security and accompanying personal fulfillment. I was 62 years old, but felt as young or younger than the 56 years fraudulently documented on the driver's license issued to Robert P. Clark in my wallet. Travel always filled me with a kind of youthful excitement. It came on me whether I was stored like a sardine on troopships crossing the Atlantic and Pacific Oceans during WWII, flying first class to Europe on business/pleasure trips or driving through the Rockies in an ill-fitting VW Bug. My pulse quickened again as I flew into Washington D.C.'s Dulles International Airport with its glistening cantilevered terminal designed by the immigrant Finnish-American architect Eero Saarinen.

My adrenaline surged even more as I sped south on I-95 in a rental car, far exceeding the posted 55 m.p.h. speed limit in an effort to reach the Richmond Professional Placement Agency on time. I got to the office of Richard Severeid very late, but this pleasant man was still able to take me to an unscheduled job interview for a tax preparation position before I checked in at my motel. The interview went well, but I never heard from that particular CPA firm again. The interview that had been scheduled in advance took place the following morning. Mr. Joyner, a senior partner in the firm of Maddrea, Joyner, Kirkham and Woody, seemed pleased with my credentials and offered me a job to start in mid-January. After talking it over with Delores, I decided to accept the job and I was excited to travel back to Richmond.

Fortunately, a real estate agent there who had helped Mr. Severeid find a house there, helped me line up temporary housing. My host, whom I shall call Wally, was a personable southern gentleman with whom I established a good and true relationship that continues to this writing. Wally had a large house and since he lived there alone he was able to rent out rooms to folks who needed temporary lodgings in Richmond. I remember his commenting to me when we first met that

I must be a good and trusting person since I sent him rental deposit check before we ever met. Although his house was not a commune in the modern Hippy sense, it certainly housed a congenial group of people. Wally let his rental guests use the kitchen and we took turns buying groceries and preparing evening meals. After I started working, I either packed a "brown bag" lunch or ate at a mall across the street from the office with restaurants that featured a variety of cuisines. My favorite place was a Chinese eatery.

The firm was a pleasant place to work. Mr. Joyner, the senior partner, was about my age. He had a quiet, courtly manner. Mr. Kirkham, a Vietnam veteran, was very friendly and loquacious. I wondered why there was one fewer partner than those listed in the name of the firm, and learned only later that the most senior partner had passed away. The surviving partners were still paying off his estate for the purchase of his share of the firm.

The secretary, Sandra Silbermann,was a Jewish lady from the Bronx. We became good friends partly, I suppose, because we didn't exactly fit in with the Old South manner of the folks we worked with. Sandra's New York accent and my Midwestern twang (which I always considered to be standard American) certainly set us apart linguistically from the others in the office. Sandra, who had three children about the same ages as mine had been, somehow inspired confidence. I found myself talking about things that I generally habitually kept to myself, such as my having grown up in Michigan, having been married before and having lived in New Jersey.

I was surprised at how few tax returns were assigned to me, and felt guilty about being paid ($24,000 per year) for doing so little work. I asked to handle some extra assignments, especially during the non-tax season. I did accompany the head partner on one audit and did some extra clerical work. Nevertheless, I felt increasingly insecure in my job, as I felt I wasn't pulling my weight in the firm. At the same time I had some doubts about the quality of my work on the returns I did handle. The difficulty I had with the Virginia state tax returns was understandable, since these tax laws were new to me. But I made more errors on the federal returns than I should have. Still the officers were always congenial in their dealings with me.

Perhaps as a hedge against losing my position, I asked for permission to resume working on my own time for H&R Block during the tax season. It was understood that I would work at a location where I wouldn't draw clients away from the firm. I got assigned to a Block office located some ten miles away but close to the house we had purchased in Delores' name in Chesterfield County. In addition, in my spare time I did some pro bono work for Wally, who had invested in a secretarial school. He and his partner needed to have accounting records put in order so as to qualify for the accreditation needed to attract people seeking to upgrade their secretarial and office skills. Unfortunately, their venture failed.

On the spiritual front, I had been attending an Evangelical Lutheran Church of America (ELCA) congregation several miles from our home and finally we joined as members in May 1989. On May 21st, there was a small get-together at the home of the pastor for those who had recently joined the church. Delores and I returned home and turned on the TV and caught the end of a show that we had seen a few times before. It was called *America's Most Wanted.* When watching the program about a month before I wondered if they would ever show a report on me. I now had an answer. At the close of the program, there was a summary of the two segments that had been shown earlier that evening. Suddenly, there I was on the screen. It was a sculpted bust that artists working from old photos some-how created to show what I would look like at the present time. It was certainly a very good likeness.

I silently wondered how many people in the Richmond would be able to match my face to the face that appeared on the most-wanted sculpture that appeared on my TV screen. I thought that if anyone did, I would surely be picked up within the next ten days. I didn't consider the fact that the program was broadcast nationally by Fox network to an audience of 20 million viewers.

One of those watching had been a neighbor of ours in Denver, Wanda Flan-ery. She had been a close friend of Delores and we had helped her in a variety of ways. I had done her tax return and got her a refund instead of her owing money to the IRS as she had expected. We had visited her in the hospital and had driven her to the store to buy groceries after she was released. But as they say: *No good deed will ever go unpunished.*

About two years earlier, Wanda had thought she recognized me as one of the FBI's 10 Most-Wanted in a photo published in World Weekly, a sensationalist tabloid sold in supermarkets. She had shown the photo to Delores, who said she was sure it was someone else and threw the paper away. I was never told of the incident. This time, Wanda was sure she recognized me and had her son place a call to the show's hotline (800-CRIME89). He first asked if there was a reward and hung up when told there was none. At Wanda's insistence, he called a second time to report the Robert Clark's address in Midlothian, Virginia, which he read off the back of an envelope that had held a recent letter from Delores.

Meanwhile, in Richmond on or about May 27, 1989, we witnessed Civil War re-enactments which I always enjoyed as a certified Civil War history and war games buff.

On the morning of June 21st, I went to work as usual. Two partners had left early to attend an accounting conference in Charlottesville. I had gone to a back room to make copies of some document, and on my way back to my office I was confronted by three men. After I was identified as Bob Clark by Sandra, the men quickly shoved me up against the wall and frisked me. They identified themselves as FBI and I realized the jig was up.

I was led to a car in the covered parking lot and put in the back seat with one of the agents while the second agent drove and the third followed in another car. On the way to a Richmond County police station my escort repeatedly urged me to admit that I was John List. I identified myself as Bob Clark and was determined to stick with this line at least until I could see an attorney. I wasn't about to make the officers' jobs any easier, even after they checked my fingerprints with on-line equipment and had my true identity confirmed beyond any reasonable doubt.

I was taken to a county courthouse and kept in a holding area before I was led to the courtroom. While there, the lady who had been our realtor came to the door to peer in at me. She shook her head and left. This should have forewarned me that the visitors' gallery would be packed with rubber-neckers whom I'd neither met nor seen before. If they expected fireworks they had to be disappointed. The judge briefly ruled that I would not receive a court appointed defense counsel, even though my income had stopped that morning. Later I was able to contact a lawyer I had retained to get compensation for an auto accident I had been involved in the previous Thanksgiving. He passed me on to another lawyer, an African American who owed him a favor and who was possibly better able to handle criminal cases. I had several conferences with this lawyer, who initially said he would fight extradition to NJ and later changed his mind, possibly because I was in no position to pay additional fees for his services. From the courtroom I was moved to a room that contained nothing but air, a floor, four walls, a ceiling and a door with a window, also, possibly a toilet and wash basin. I was clad in a paper thin gown such as used in hospitals. I felt chills, as the shock of my situation sunk in with numbing effect, and I curled up in a fetal position to keep as warm as possible on the cold linoleum floor. I later got a mattress and a blanket. The eyes of a stranger at the window kept me under constant surveillance, presumably to see that I wouldn't harm myself.

After several meetings with attorneys, arrangements were made for my transfer to New Jersey. Among my escorts was the retired Chief of Police of Westfield, who was givn the honor of placing handcuffs on me. He asked me if I knew who he was and I allowed that I hadn't the foggiest notion. Apparently this was the highlight of his professional life and he was praised by the media for his diligence. He had refused to close the book on my case, and I only escaped the long arm of the law for eighteen years.

On the way to the airport, my caravan passed through an area jam packed with members of the Fourth Estate, which resembled nothing more than a school of piranhas. A lady said she had a coat I could place over my head, but my lawyer and I both declined the offer. I wanted to be able to walk in as natural a manner as possible under the circumstances. I maintained my composure as we encountered another swarm of journalists at the Richmond airport. They shouted questions at me as they ran backwards in the manner of a defensive back in the NFL.

I was taken to a room away from the general traffic area and was allowed to make a personal telephone call. On board the aircraft, I got a window seat with two of my escorts seated on the middle and aisle seats. My cuffs were removed in accordance with airline regulations. When we arrived in Newark, we got off after all the other passengers had disembarked and we joined a multi-car convoy headed for the Union County jail in Elizabeth, and the trial that would end the twisted saga of my life in the maximum security New Jersey State Prison.

Reflections of Wally, Bob Clark's friend in Richmond, VA.:

Bob and I shared a common interest in history in general and Civil War history in particular and became rather close friends. On one occasion, Bob spoke of his past, mentioned that his first wife had died of cancer, and that he had looked after her daughter when she got into some kind of trouble. Just hen Bob abruptly clammed up and acted like he suddenly realized that he was talking too much.

Although Bob struck me as a highly intelligent and well-mannered gentleman, he occasionally came across as a bit strange. Both Betty., who met Bob socially several times, and I shared the feeling that Bob was somehow too nice, too kind and too considerate of others to qualify as a normal human being. For example, he told me that the main reason he had moved to Richmond was to please Delores, who was unhappy in Denver and wanted to live closer to her relatives on the east coast. As it worked out, her life in the Richmond area has been anything but a happy one. Driven into near seclusion by media hounding, I understand she exists on a bare subsistence income.

Reflections of Jerome Kendall, fellow Lutheran church member in Richmond, VA:

My impression of Bob is that, contrary to the monster he has been portrayed to be in the newspapers, he is in fact as ordinary an individual as I have ever met. [He was] beset at one time or another with the same sorts of problems—job, money, family, society in general—as anyone else. He worked at Xerox, I worked at Xerox. He liked to read. I liked to read. He likes chess, I like chess. We have been playing two games concurrently via the mail for years.

10

Life in Prison

So here we are at the dawn of a new Millenium, and I'm in late afternoon of my third life as a marginal presence on Planet Earth.

In my 80th year, I'm warehoused in the ordered confines of the cell assigned to me, convict number 226472, at the New Jersey State Prison in Trenton. This is a maximum security institution inhabited mostly by lifers sent up to pay their debt to society incurred by their violent actions, removed from the mainstream of society lest they reprise the crimes that led to their incarceration. I don't really fit the mould, for I'm anything but a person predisposed to violence. In fact, it was probably my lack of aggressively competitive genes that caused me to fall short of achieving my career and material goals in the dog-eat-dog world in which I was born and, eventually, broken. On the other hand, there's no doubt that I did carry out violent actions when I shot and killed my wife, mother and three teen-aged children more than thirty years ago.

The memory of what I did on that pivotal day in my life has ever since haunted me, filled me with remorse and a consuming need to pray for forgiveness by a just and loving God.

Here in prison I have found plenty of time to pray, both privately in the confines of a room just large enough for a cot, toilet, wash basin, chair and desk, and in spiritual communion with visiting pastors and fellow Christians. For this I am truly grateful. My old 86th Blackhawk Division comrade, "Red" Goodrich, once asked me how I would like to exchange greetings with God at the gates of heaven. Here's how I answered him:

First, I would refer to St. Paul's statement in one of his letters, in which he said that he was "the chief of sinners" because of his conduct while persecuting Christians. I feel that I must have displaced him as chief sinner because of the dreadful murders that I committed. Therefore, I know that I can only enter heaven because of the tremendous grace and love of humanity that God has for us.

Then I would be most happy to have God say to me, "Enter heaven chief of sinners because you accepted my son's suffering and death as the substitute for all of your sins."

I shall then be most happy to be assigned to the lowest rank in heaven because of my unworthiness.

Meanwhile, I struggle to ward off the ennui of hopelessness that accompanies prison life, poised to spread its mind-numbing effect like early morning mists on a millpond. I observe all around me how repetitive routines spawned by conditions of imprisonment serve to erode the mental processes that separate us from the animal kingdom. Aware of this danger, I defend against it by keeping mentally active. I know that I should be more physically active as well, but I've never been any great shakes in that department, and frankly I'm wary of spending more time in the yard than I have to because of the physical confrontations, up to and including murder that take place out there in the otherwise healthy fresh air.

In any case, there's my diabetes, which was first diagnosed in prison and for which I now receive two shots of insulin every day. This limits the amount of physical exercise I can handle, and it may have been a factor that influenced my murderous behavior. My otherwise competent defense counsel, Elijah Miller, must have known of research that has related diabetes to the commission of violent crime but for whatever reason, he failed to introduce my diabetes, as well as my *post traumatic stress disorder* resulting from WWII combat, as material to my defense.

In addition to Bible study courses and work in reorganizing prison files, for which I am paid enough to buy stamps and Christmas presents for friends and relatives on the outside, I have enjoyed the fellowship provided by religious services and meetings of the convicts' military veterans club. I am grateful for the prson administration for permitting, even encouraging, these activities. I am also thankful for permission given me to get a word processor paid for with contributions earmarked for this purpose by my old Army comrades. This has helped to provide me with the mental stimulation needed to survive as a human being in prison. More than that, this electronic handmaiden of the information age provides me with a precious sense of freedom inherent in the act of self-expression preserved and stored in a memory far superior to my own. In short, my word processor has become an essential part of my life, a good buddy who enables me to escape for hours at a time from the world-shrinking debilitation of prison life. Perhaps Descartes' dictum "I think, therefore I am," needs to be extended to include the electronic functions in which contemporary thought is encased, stimulated, facilitated and preserved. (I can't put that into Latin.) Or do these extensions merely serve as unnecessary window dressing?

In response to a request by my old platoon mate, "Red" Goodrich, I'll sit down and express some of the best and worst things about prison life. I hope my off-the-cuff observations will shed some light on my reason for being and provide some sort of framework for a more detailed examination of my life and crimes. Like dessert, I'll save the best for last. So what's so bad about prison life?

The Bad Stuff

The area known as "The Hole" is bad. It's a wing in the prison in which there are about 100 cells, each measuring about six by ten feet. But it's not the cell's size that makes it bad (I had the same size when I first came here), it's the conditions there. First, there are no creature comforts such as the TVs and radios found in regular cells. Cells in the Hole are furnished with a bed, washbasin and toilet. Perod. Illumination is provided by a single light that is left on 24/7. This makes sleep difficult, but that's a normal condition, because starting in the evening there's a cacophony of shouted conversations among inmates up and down the line. In fact, some prisoners have been known to deliberately break the rules so as to be sent to the Hole where they can exchange news with old friends there.

I was sent to the Hole in the spring of 1995 as punishment for an alleged violation of the rules. My wife, Delores, and I had just completed a visit and I was a few seconds slow in getting out of the meeting room and into the prisoner's holding area. Just as I reached the sliding door it slammed shut in my face. I knocked in vain to get in and was told to go to another gate to be strip-searched. That meant I was to go to the Hole. An official advised me that I was charged with *attempt to escape*. When I refused to plead guilty to that, the charge was reduced to *out of place*, which still produced a sentence of a week in the Hole. Apparently, some guard had it in for me, because I was told later that when I didn't get out of the visiting hall in time, one of the guards proudly told another guard "We got List." Afterwards, whenever I met this man in the halls I made a point of looking him square in the eye, but he always avoided eye contact.

Lock downs are another bad event in prisons. They happen whenever an act of violence has occurred necessitating a search of prisoners and our "condos." During a lock down, there is no prisoner movement without escorts, all work is suspended and we get meals brought to our cells. I get my insulin shot by a nurse in my cell. A lock down can last from one day to several weeks.

We were once locked down (imprisoned in a prison, if you will) after a guard was stabbed by an inmate as an act of revenge in a prison in Camden. According to the in-house grapevine, which transmits information at a speed that would make the internet appear slow as molasses, the guard had objected to the noise made by a couple of homosexuals when they did their thing in the cell they shared. Finally, one of the inmates was moved to another "condo" and his partner murdered the guard whom he held responsible for their involuntary separation.

During this lock down the second guard shift refused to go on duty until the Governor promised to supply armored vests to all guards. When the bullet-proof vests arrived, many of the guards declined to wear then because of their heat. One lock down caused by convicts attacking guards in the Control Center lasted 12 days. Our cells were searched from floor to ceiling to find *shanks*, prisonspeak for any homemade weapon, usually made from a toothbrush handle or metal spoon that could be used for stabbing. (I lost many personal articles during that search including a hearing aid, which it took some time to have replaced.) Old fashioned tooth brushes have been banned, replaced by brushes attached a soft handle. Fortunately, I bought up a supply of conventional handles so that I had a cache of 20 in reserve.

Cutting shanks that used razor blades led to a prohibition against double-track razors. Only BIC disposable, which nick my skin, are permitted. Armed with foresight, I bought up enough extra blades to keep me supplied for the next two years. (To save on blades I shave only once every three days.)

Of the non-violent bad things in prison, I have to mention an act of poor judgment on my part that stemmed from the best of intentions. Ever since my incarceration began I had a burning desire to somehow in some measure compensate my wife, Delores, for all the suffering I had caused her by my deception. The unrelenting pressure put on her by the representative of what is nobly called Fourth Estate can best be labeled media rape. I blame these people, even though it is I who should be blamed for marrying my wife under false pretenses. How could I atone for deception that had caused my totally innocent wife so much suffering? The $4.00 per day I received for my work in the Records Center wouldn't provide much compensation. Finally my attention fell on an opportunity to shorten the odds for winning a big sweepstakes put by subscribing to a newsletter. For only a nominal $10 annual fee plus postage costs I could enter hundreds of Sweepstakes. With the help of friends on the outside I entered countless contests at a cost of more than $1,000 in postage, which produced zero winnings. Later I learned that any winnings would have been taken by the state of New Jersey in payment for my Public Defender legal expenses of roughly a quarter of a million Reichsbucks!

The bad things about prison life are actually minor inconveniences compared with the essential loss of physical freedom. What a precious right, that we take for granted. Of course freedom is never absolute. As Chief Justice Holmes observed, the freedom of speech guaranteed in the First Amendment does not guarantee the freedom of a person to shot "FIRE" in a crowded theatre. Still, when one considers the restrictive rules and regulations imposed by governments and cultural traditions that mock individual freedom in most countries, we Americans are remarkably free. We're free to do and say what we please, wear clothes of our choice, travel wherever we wish. TO be denied these freedoms, particularly the freedom to meet with loved ones, has to be the worst single aspect of life in prison. This is true even for me, the product of a well-ordered family life structured to insulate me from the outside world. Yes, on reflection…

I suppose I was somewhat less free than most of my generation, because I was the only child of loving German Lutheran parents who believed in raising me in accordance with the strict rules of a god-fearing Christian home. Thus, biblical commandments were accepted unconditionally without the need for harsh punishment. (I can only remember being spanked twice, once by each of my parents, for bad behavior and for speaking disrespectfully of a family friend. Naturally, I was never permitted to take the Lord's name in vain or use any kind of profanity. This was easy because my parents never swore, and my contact with kids who used foul language was minimal. Children of my age raised in less disciplined homes grew up in quite a different social setting. They pulled all kinds of antisocial stunts in celebration of the pagan practices of Halloween. On one occasion, some of these kids were pulling pranks outside our house when my father chased them away, much to my embarrassment and isolation from what I suppose represented mainstream youth in 1930's Bay City, Michigan. It didn't help that one of the kids got hurt while fleeing from my father's righteous wrath.

On reflection, I have to admit that the well-ordered life of my childhood prepared me well for the hidebound discipline of Army life, the only slightly less restrictive rules of college life and, finally, into the static world of numbers in the accounting profession. By extension, I suppose that my basic personality and upbringing served to cushion the more or less traumatic shocks rendered by life in prison.

I probably would have been a model citizen living under the authoritarian regimes imposed by the communist rulers in Eastern Europe. Indeed, I can understand the stress felt by generations who had lived under Communism when suddenly the liberation tney had prayed for suddenly became reality. (Better be careful what you wish for!) It must have been like being thrown out into the jungle where there were no rules, where survival meant having to cope with the lions and tigers who were stronger, faster and hungrier than oneself. Under communism, fascism or any other closed system, people exchange the uncertain benefits of freedom for the comfortable assurance that basic needs—housing, medical care and three square meals a day will be met. Just like prison.

Still, if given the choice, I'd have to opt for the uncertainties of freedom. Unfortunately, I don't have a choice, since a sentence of five consecutive life terms means that I won't be eligible for parole for another century or so.

As much as I miss freedom of movement, I miss at least as much its corollary, the opportunity to get together with relatives and close friends. In the absence of meeting these folks face to face, I guess the next best thing would be to talk with them via the Ameche, the slang name we gave the telephone after actor Don Ameche, who played Alexander Graham Bell in the movie about the device's inventor.

Unfortunately, it's not like stepping into a phone booth, depositing a coin and dialing a number. We don't have telephones in the rooms of this motel, but we are permitted to make calls under certain conditions. Outgoing calls must be approved in advance, however, which means that a mutually convenient date and time must be arranged with one's correspondent by mail and coordinated with the prison authorities. When the connection is finally made, the conditions of the conversation are hardly conducive to a casual exchange of thoughts and feelings. After an exchange of greetings, and expressions of love, what is there to say that won't be mutually boring, hurtful or both. Perhaps a TV show seen by both parties could be discussed, but even this possibility is limited by the absence of cable television here at the Inn. Surely the party on the outside is less than thrilled to hear about the stultifying routines of prison life. And the caller on the inside feels more hurt than joy to hear of pleasurable experiences beyond his reach in a world that exists only in his reverie. Each tick of the clock brings with it a depressing sense of guilt on the part of the inmate, whose call must be put on his correspondent's phone bill. Finally, there's always the intimidating possibility of prison personnel eavesdropping on the conversations that might possibly involve drug deals. (Despite all of the measures designed to prevent drug trafficking in the big house, this illicit commerce still flourishes. I wonder how?)

In October 1997, a new regulation went into effect that permitted us to make calls only by signing up for a personal identification (PIN) number, which involved identifying our correspondents and giving the authorities the unconditional right to listen in on and record our conversations. Opposition to this new system was led by an inmate named John, who served in an orientation group working with new prisoners. He advised all newcomers to refuse to relinquish what was left of their privacy rights by signing up for a PIN.

It turned out that John had his own means of circumventing the rules. While he was having a contact visit in early December, guards appeared in the visiting area and unceremoniously hauled him off to the hole. Word went out that a cellular phone had been found in John's cell when the concealed instrument revealed its presence by ringing within earshot of a guard. Later we learned that this was a cover story designed to protect an informant who had snitched on John. In any case, the area in which the NOKIA man worked was closed for several days to permit a thorough search to find more of the devices used to communicate secretly with the outside world.

How could a cell phone get through the rigorous inspection of all parcels coming into the prison? Perhaps in the same way that drugs somehow manage to get through holes in the same security net.

One would think that boredom spawned by mind-numbing routines would rank high on the list of the ills of prison life. At the risk of appearing illogical, I have to disagree. To me, unexpected changes in daily routines carried out in fixed locations are far more upsetting. I avoid boredom by keeping active, but it is important that this activity be accomplished within fixed boundaries. Thus, I write letters, exercise, have my devotions, eat, sleep, get my insulin shots, attend meetings and even take naps at fixed intervals. I simply like it this way. That's why I got terribly upset by unscheduled events that happened in October, 1996. Here's what I wrote at the time:

After insoluble problems with my Adler-Royal word processor, I was able to get enough money together to buy a new model Smith-Corona. But before I could buy this new machine, I had to get rid of the old one. I sent out the typewriter unit to a church group which sends us food packages and other forms of support. Then the fun began. On October 16th, I received a notice from the Mail Room that my word processor had been "refused." The notice was dated the 10th and I don't know what took them so long to get it to me. Anyway, I decided to write to the retailer and explain the problem; namely, that the box was too large, larger than the original carton used by the manufacturer. But before I got it mailed, on my way to a meeting I was stopped at the 3DD Control Booth and lo and behold: there was my word processor. Apparently, it had been re-shipped to meet the in-house requirements without my intervention. I guess that sometimes good things happen to those who simply sit and wait.

On the following two days I learned how to operate the new unit with the help of a man who had recently gotten the same model. Then I got word that we would be moved to different cells. On October 26th, word spread along the grapevine that we would all be moved the next day. I didn't quite believe it, but on the next day the first men started to be moved out. It was terrible. I had grown accustomed to the cell I'd occupied for more than six years. But then, on October 30, 1996, the announcement was made: MOVE CANCELLED. Halleluiah! We're not moving. I found out when I went down for lunch. It was such a relief. I had felt bad physically as well as mentally. Now I felt much better.

My shortest move occurred on February 8, 1991, when a problem in the lock on my door I feared might cause me to be sent to the ancient West Compound, which I wanted to avoid at all costs. I suggested that I simply move to the adjoining cell during the day, but this reasonable proposal met with knee-jerk rejection. A guard told me that in refusing my proposal the officer in Central Control had explained he had no intention of jeopardizing his pension in case there was a fire and I, trapped in my cell, would be incinerated. Wasn't that touching?

The clinching argument from the powers that be held that if I didn't agree to move to another location, I'd be sent to the *hole*. I'd been there, done that, and I'd just as soon not return.

As it turned out, a practice run search of room #34 by a new class of guards had turned up something illegal in the room of the nice, quiet man who lived there, and he was sent to the hole. His ill fortune was a blessing to me, since it made it possible for me to move right next door. Room ##$ was a mirror image of #35, which took some getting use to and involved my having to re-string my laundry drying lines. But all the problems were little ones, including little bugs called cockroaches, who unlike humanoids seem to thrive in a prison environment. Cell #34 had been inadequately roach-proofed, so I had to take the pesticide measures I had earlier carried out to sanitize my old room. Again, I called on Frank Pennington to mix up a batch of his roach-proofing concoction, consisting of toilet paper, water and Elmer's glue. I thought as Frank mixed his magical ingredients that prisons surely are the mothers of invention, or "field expedients" as we caked improvised problem solving in the Army. When properly kneaded, the glue, water and toilet paper formed a putty-like substance which could be used to seal up all the cracks in walls and floors. A greater problem was posed by my cardboard boxes used to store documents, including copies of correspondence, legal papers and the like. The street smart skills of the roaches enable them to use the frayed edges and corners in these boxes as breeding grounds, where they could lay their eggs and train their filthy little offsprings in the art of spreading germs to infect their human prey. I had to try to patch these little roach hotels as best I could with scotch tape and glue. The best solution was to use plastic containers, but these had to be purchased, and the price, including shipping and handling, was more than I could afford. I later obtained five 56-quart containers and two 44-quart containers, which put me over the limit of five to a customer. But several other men were over their limit, too, which makes me believe that our custodians may bend the roles a bit at times in the interest of maintaining their charges' morale at an acceptable level.

After the roach-proofing was completed, another of the convicts' network of skilled tradesmen, a fellow named Don Naples, came in to paint my living quarters. Originally the walls were done in light blue with a burgundy trim for the windows and shelves. Don had earlier twice covered the walls of my room with white, but the blue still showed through in places. The third coat was a charm: the trim was transformed into a pleasant medium gray, and the walls became so starkly white that I used to joke about having to wear sunglasses while working at my word processor.

There are some prison experiences I recall as neither bad nor good but sort of in between. For example, during my introduction to incarceration, at Elizabeth County jail, I experienced the mixed blessing of being a high profile prisoner. It was nice to have a private room, but on the downside the hallway outside my cell was used by civilians visiting the place to do some sightseeing. I guess I was the sight they had come to see.

When I first arrived at this jail, a lady took my medical history. Several days later, she returned to have me sign the papers again, because someone had torn off my original signature. I wonder how much an original List autograph would command in today's market.

In a similar vein, my photo ID, which normally was kept in a rack in the front office, kept disappearing. After several such disappearances I was told to keep my badge instead of turning it in after using it in limited areas where we were permitted to be without escort guard.

Another indication of my high profile status emerged during my short stay at Yardville, a reception center for prisoners entering the state penal system. It was here that prisoners took showers, were photographed, issued new clothes and issued a new ID badge and penal number. Most men enjoyed the laid-back atmosphere at Yardville for a coup0le of weeks before being moved on to a state prison. As a high profile prisoner, I was there for only a couple of hours before being driven in a car followed by a private escort vehicle to Trenton.

Shortly after my arrival at my final destination, an experienced guard took me aside and told me that because of my advanced age and my notoriety I would be well advised to sign up for Protective Custody PC. This was good advice. But once again it was a mixed blessing. On the one hand it provided me some time to acclimatize to prison life without risk of assault by another inmate for whatever reason. But at the same time the PC accommodations were a few cuts below those offered at the Waldorf. The cell was about 4.5 feet wide and 7.5 feet long with steel walls and furnishings consisting of a cot and a footlocker. Period. Worst of all the room was located on the top floor, some 15 feet beneath a steel that served as a n oven broiler. By mid-May when I arrived, the heat was stifling, and by mid-June it became so hot that I don't know how I could have survived if I hadn't been able to buy a fan with funds provided by my good and loyal wife, Delores. With heat that made my Army exposure to summer weather in Louisiana and the Philippines seem arctic by comparison, I spent most of the time lying on my cot wearing only skivvies with the fan blowing directly on me.

The only way to escape the heat of my cell was to go out into the yard, a concrete paved area about half the size of a football field for an hour and a half of exercise in the afternoon. There I met several men who have been good friends ever since, including one who cut my hair, one who made a special TV ear plug for me so I could listen to my TV without disturbing others, and Steve Mozer, who was a great help in preparing my judicial appeals. Which brings me to:

The Good Stuff

Human kindness. On the face of it, this quality might seem to be out of place among the social outcasts living in abrasively close quarters inside a maximum security prison. But it may be that this setting, bad as it is, may create the perfect environment for the serving of spiritual food because conditions are shared by all of us equally. Stripped of material goods and all of the thoughts and emotions that accompany their acquisition, we are transformed into a society of equals—a form of pure communism if you will—where we have to find satisfaction and eventual salvation by letting into our lives the goodness with which we are all endowed by God. As we perforce share each other's pain, we experience humbling compassion, true love. I've hear it said that South Asian Indians judge a person's moral worth by the way he or she treats animals, because animals cannot repay kindness in any material way. Virtue must be its own reward. I believe that this applied to human relationships in prison where we are in a real sense like animals in a fenced yard. Random acts of kindness happen, more often than one might think, and by repetition become habitual and create a sort of (dare I say it?) honorable prison ethos.

I experienced the unlikely presence of Christian charity at an early stage of my incarceration when I first moved into my cell in Trenton. I was among a group of prisoners who were directed to their quarters where they were to spend most or all of the rest of their lives. We were quietly greeted by our new neighbors, who gave us pencils, writing paper, stamps and other tangible evidence of solidarity, shared compassion. When I told one of my benefactors that I would repay his kindness as soon as I could, I was told: *Never mind, just do the same for some other new arrival here at the Inn.*

Occasionally the milk of human kindness even flows from our custodians. For example, n January 22, 1993, I noticed an ugly red rash on my chest and stomach. When I showed this to the nurse who administered my insulin shots, she immediately had me see a doctor. After several different pills and ointments had no effect, the nurse who takes my monthly blood samples got Dr. Goyos from Columbia, Latin America, to see me. He eliminated several of the medications I was getting and I was released from the infirmary on February 1st.

I had received good care. Equally important to me was how for several weeks afterwards the nurses and some guards inquired after the state of my health. They didn't have to do that.

◆   ◆   ◆

It is said there are no atheists in foxholes. I believe this, and I would add that in my experience there are precious few if any non-believers in prison. I have been amazed by how many of my fellow inmates whom I had thought to be hard-core criminal types are knowledgeable people of faith. I've also been surprised by the number of prisoners who have been quite willing to talk about their innermost religious convictions with me.

Maybe I should have gone into the ministry as my Pastor once suggested back in my high schooldays. I do feel comfortable discussing religion with my friends here, and perhaps I would have been able to provide counseling that might have kept them on the straight and narrow and outside these brick walls. More importantly, a pastoral career would most certainly have kept me from committing the terrible sins that landed me here.

Still, religion continues to play a central role in my life, and I nourish my spirit with a more or less fixed program of study and prayer every single day.

On Sunday, after listening to the Lutheran Hour radio broadcast, I start my own solo service, which follows one of four orders of worship service, which I rotate. I read four hymns that are appropriate for each Sunday taken from the hymnal used by the Lutheran Church Missouri Synod (LCMS). Then I read a sermon, either one of those I received from Pastor Warther while I was in the Elizabeth County jail, or one of Martin Luther's sermons that appear in a two-volume edition that I have in my treasury. My services are about 45 minutes, somewhat shorter than a normal church service since I need not take time to collect offerings.

My weekday devotionals are an important part of my daily routine. First, after attending to my toilet, I begin a devotional period that may be interrupted but never replaced by having to go for my insulin shot or breakfast. I use a prayer that I have developed over the past decades based on a one-page outline. During this prayer that takes about five minutes, I pray for my friends, relatives, myself and other persons with special needs. I change this prayer about every six months to keep abreast of changing situations. Some parts are not subject to revision, including my appeal for God to bless my wife Delores and her relatives, and all members of our military services, especially those who are held hostages, are homeless or displaced.

I then turn to a prayer book that has prayers for each morning and afternoon of the week. These readings I alternate with prayers taken from Portals of Prayer, published by Concordia Publishers. I then read the Lord's Prayer, the Apostles Creed and about two pages from the Bible. I sometimes supplement my bible readings with writings in Norman Vincent Peale's monthly GUIDEPOSTS, which has articles by people who have survived some threatening experience in a miraculous manner.

After returning from work around 10 a.m., I say a prayer primarily for my wife Dee and myself. When IU get back from my job in the Forms Room in the afternoon, I normally take a shower and do my laundry, have a half pint of milk and an orange or such before getting into the next devotions, for which I use that morning's outline. This I supplement with the "Our Daily Bread" devotional that I get from the Radio Bible Class in Grand Rapids, Michigan. I have some Christian readings before supper, and complete my devotions with a prayer from the day's outline before the eleven o'clock TV news. If I've fallen asleep, I may have to postpone my evening prayer until I awake, often around midnight.

I don't mean to leave the impression that my religious life in prison is a solitary pursuit. The pastors who have visited me, provided counseling and administered the sacrament of communion deserve my heartfelt gratitude. I should also mention the loving service of a little old nun named Sister Sofia, who led our seniors group in the early 90's. In her mid 80's, this sprightly servant of God brought light into our lives for an hour or so once or twice a week. She sometimes smuggled in candy, mostly the sugar-free variety for the benefit of me and another diabetic. Sister Sophia, who among many other things taught the Italian language in England and the English language in Italy fell and broke one or more bones during her ministry to us, but this never kept her away for long. She was determined to see *her men*, as she called us.

But What if…what if I were to be released from prison next week? I have actually given that some thought in my reverie. Generally I would want to go somewhere that doesn't have temperature extremes. Places that would appear on my short list would include Denver, even though it's a bit cold there in the winter, Colorado Springs or Pueblo, Colorado. Also, I'd include an area in south central Colorado known as the Banana belt for its pleasant year-round climate. Somewhere in the northern part of Arizona, where it gets cool in the higher elevations might be nice to spend my sunset years, as would several places along the Pacific coast.

The longest shot for retirement, hands down, would be Ulithi Atoll, where our troop ship anchored for a couple of days en route to the Philippines at the close of WWII. That was heat in the extreme. I recall that the entire ship became a huge oven that baked troops clad in olive drab boxer shorts crammed into the welded steel quarters below deck. Deck space was at a premium, but you had to stake out your two by four foot "turf" at night because in the sun, the deck became one large skillet.

To retire anywhere outside these prison walls I would have had to live my life over again. This leads to self-criticism, an important element in *group dynamics* sessions, just as *auto critique* is a requirement in communist party cells, and regular confessions, constitute an essential element of Roman Catholic practice.

So let's take a look in the rear view mirror. First, I learned too late the importance of being flexible, adaptable in managing my professional life. Why did I never explore or consider alternative avenues in my professional career? Why couldn't I branch out from the narrow paths generally followed by accountants?

In my personal life, I should have been less flexible and stuck to my belief that sexual abstinence was the right way to go before marriage. That would have prevented a lot of later troubles. On the other hand, when my partner realized that contrary to what she had thought, she was not pregnant, I should have called a halt to marriage plans based on her assumed condition. But I was too inflexible to consider alternative courses of action.

Also I should have been more flexible when I returned to the Army during the Korean War. After I had been at Ft. Mason for a time in the Finance Department of the Controllers Division, I was asked if I would like to transfer to the Personnel Department of that division. I turned down the offer out of hand because I felt that my background was in accounting and finance and I didn't want to be sidetracked. I should have been open minded enough to at least consider a position that would have broadened my knowledge and experience. And, incidentally, access to some lovely young ladies working in Personnel.

In this same vein, one of my superior officers had asked me to consider applying for a commission in the Regular Army. Again, I turned it down without exploring the benefits of a long-term career in the Army. Later, when I was released from my tour of duty in 1952, I should have retained an Active Reserve status in order to keep open an alternative career path. The trouble was that I was all too certain that I would be assured of success in the business world, where I should have realized, the dog-eat-dog competition was about as far as one could get from my staid upbringing. By the time I realized that my square personality simply did not fit in the round hole of the business world, I had been deactivated from the Army Reserves. In the 1960's I wrote to the Army asking if my commission status could be reactivated, but it was too late. The Pentagon said no.

And what happened happened.

This might be as good a point as any to introduce some of my friends here at the Inn. They have kindly agreed to share their views on prison life in general and their evaluation of John List in particular without input or editing by me.

Comments by George J. Corbett

There is absolutely no rehabilitation in the U.S. prison system. It's like your living the same day over and over again...You begin to realize that you grow apart from your family. It gets to the point where they come to visit and after 10 minutes you're looking at each other trying to think of something to say.

On John List

I like John and I enjoy conversing with him. To evaluate him, I can only say that he is intelligent and very organized. He's thoughtful too. He saves food and juices for me. John List is a good person who once did a really bad thing...

I felt bad for John when I overheard someone wish him a happy father's day. That made me realize that he must have a lot to carry around with himself emotionally.

Comments by Steven Mozer #219247

There is no experience that can prepare one for the anathema that is incarceration. One's dignity is left at the proverbial door, and any man with any sense of manhood is viewed with contempt and unequivocally targeted as a threat...If heaven and hell can be states of mind, incarceration relegates one to a perpetual purgatory.

On John List

I do not consider it appropriate to contemplate the tragedy that struck his life, save to comment that I opine the events that led to this misfortune, and the misfortune of his family, could not possibly be repeated. I believe that he acted out of a legitimate sense of honoring his duty to the Lutheran Church and that he was, through self-sacrifice, acting for the great good of the souls of his family. Perchance termed altruism, however misguided.

Comments by Daryl L. Pitts #795669

After 17 years here, including four and a half years on death row, I've watched my family and "friends" (a term that is loosely used) disappear. They all become a fading memory that you hold onto as long as possible but sooner or later reality sets in and you can't lie to yourself anymore. You have to tell yourself one day "wake the fuck up, they are only a distant memory." The purpose of state-inflicted pain is to turn a person by his screams and by his submission into a lower animal, in the eyes of all and in his own eyes.

On John List

He has always been respectful and carries himself well. I've always spoken to him with the respect that one human should give another, and he has returned the compliment. I have studied Post-Traumatic Stress Disorder for years, and I believe that John suffers from many of the symptoms.

Comments by Patrick R. Lanzel #115342

At first it's scary. Being with strangers in a hostile environment with unpublished official and inmate sets of rules is intimidating…after several years, in the absence of meaningful contact and relations with "normal" people, a part of you simply dies.

On John List

Upon first meeting John, he was friendly, but seemed very serious…However, once through that outer shell, I found John to be a kind-hearted, warm and friendly man. His wry sense of humor, intelligence and giving nature make it a pleasure to be with him and to discuss a multitude of subjects. At the core, John List is one of the finest men I have ever met. True, honest, reliable, patient and a good Christian. I am proud to call him friend.

Comments by Richard D'Agostino #79030

Prisons are inherently mysterious, dangerous settings. More and more people seem to be interested in the brutality of prison life and all manner of punishment meted out behind fortress like walls and razor wire enclosures. Believe me, every day there's a Greek tragedy played out on one cellblock or another.

Beating the insane defenseless inmates (when handcuffed and shackled) is the blood sport of choice. Those sad, sad souls with eyes perpetually downcast in a fog of indifference wander the polished corridors wearing plastic slippers made in China. Communing with demons through screams—while the battle between fuzzy reality and the bizarre images marching across the walls and ceilings goes on. One day they hope to read a book or write a letter to mother. But there's no hope, none at all. They slide along the hallways with their shoulders pressed against the walls…

Must be silent—shhhhh—must not complain, must not talk, or they will come running…with clubs—and the needle.

On John List

As for my friend, John List, well, he's an extremely sensitive man holding onto social values of a time quickly passing into history. I've come to know him better, deeper since the beginning of our Post Traumatic Stress Disorder sessions. We are both combat veterans (he in WWII, I with the 4th Marines in Chu Lai in 1965.) I've discovered how similar our fears and trepidations were then and still are to this day…

Comments by Frank Pennington #55867

Prison life today is nowhere near the real prison of years gone by. In a way it's better, because there's less violence. Where we used to have 3-4 fights a day, now there are only3-4 fights a week. But there's much less respect and trust among prisoners and I sometimes wish the old days were here once again.

On John List

I met John List in 1990 after I had been released from death row. We seemed to click right away and have been friends ever since. I find John to be a man of his word and of God. He is faithful to God and when asked to do a favor, he is there.

Comments by David M. Russo #2008920

I thought the physical demands of Basic Training in the Air Force were tough…But nothing in my life prepared me for the despair, the chilling loneliness and utter desolation that a prison cell would bring to my life. Whether you're caught up in the system as a short-term prisoner or doing life, prison is the slowest and more acutely painful and wasteful place for any living thing to be warehoused in.

On John List

I've found John to be pretty darned intelligent, especially with math and financial matters. He's also a generous person. For example, he shares his magazines, including Smithsonian, National Geographic and Science Today with everyone. That may sound trivial, but you'd be surprised how much value prisoners place on informative material like this.

978-0-595-39536-1
0-595-39536-8

Made in United States
North Haven, CT
20 October 2022